Open for Business

ED A. HEWETT

with

Clifford G. Gaddy

Open for Business

Russia's Return to the Global Economy

THE BROOKINGS INSTITUTION
Washington, D.C.

Library of Congress Cataloging-in-Publication data:

Hewett, Edward A.
    Open for business : Russia's return to the global economy / Ed A.
Hewett with Clifford G. Gaddy.
        p.   cm.
    Includes bibliographical references and index.
    ISBN 0-8157-3620-7 (cloth : alk. paper) — ISBN 0-8157-3619-3
(pbk. : alk. paper)
    1. Soviet Union—Commercial policy.   2. Soviet Union—Eco-
nomic policy—1986–1991.   3. Russia (Federation)—Commercial
policy.   4. Former Soviet republics—Commercial policy.   I. Gaddy,
Clifford G.   II. Title.
HF1557.H478   1992
382'.3'0947—dc20   92-20941
                                                                  CIP

9 8 7 6 5 4 3 2 1

The paper used in this publication meets the minimum requirements of the
American National Standard for Information Sciences—Permanence of paper for Printed Library Materials, ANSI Z39.48-1984

Foreword

In December 1991 the Union of Soviet Socialist Republics—born in violent revolution and dominated for more than six decades by highly authoritarian rule—was dissolved by its constituent republics. The causes of this remarkable event will be probed for many years to come. Our understanding of it may never be complete. Nevertheless, it is evident even now that part of the story lay in a conscious redirection of policy by specific individuals. Those at the center of political and economic power understood the flaws in their system well enough to initiate a process of reform, but one that triggered a more massive transformation than they had intended.

The process has left enormous turmoil in its wake. Political power has dissipated in all the new states emerging from the fragmented former USSR, and all are struggling to establish constitutional order. They do so under conditions of severe austerity as they seek to reconstruct their once integrated, highly concentrated, internationally isolated economy into independent instruments of national viability. With no detailed blueprint available, and with only fractured mechanisms of policy control at their disposal, these new nations are being carried along by the inertia of state enterprises and by a spontaneous process of regeneration at the grass-roots level.

This book, which analyzes Gorbachev's foreign economic strategy, provides a window for understanding the disintegrative forces that stymied his reforms and eventually defeated him, undermining the country he sought to preserve. Gorbachev was committed to ending Soviet isolation from the world economy and at the same time saving

Soviet socialism. Ironically, it is the destruction of Soviet socialism, and the emergence of new post-Soviet states, that has begun to break down the isolationist barriers erected over the last seven decades. This book documents the incredibly complex legacies that Russia and the other new post-Soviet states face as they seek to integrate themselves into the global economy.

Perhaps befitting the convoluted nature of the subject matter, the history of this book is itself unusual. At the time he conceived, did the research, and wrote the first draft, Ed A. Hewett was a senior fellow in the Foreign Policy Studies program at Brookings. When he moved to his current position in the government, it was anticipated that the project could be brought to completion in his absence, with only the technical aspects of publication—verification, editing, and so on—remaining. However, by late 1991, it was clear that events in the USSR called for a more substantial revision if the book was to remain a relevant commentary on the ongoing reforms. It was decided that Clifford Gaddy, who had in the meantime taken over Hewett's portfolio at Brookings, would continue the project and assume full responsibility for the final published version.

Gaddy's goal was to retain as much as possible of Hewett's intellectual contribution and, to the extent that modifications and extensions were required, to remain true to Hewett's original concept. At the same time, it is to be emphasized that all the judgments, conclusions, and recommendations stated in this book are those made by Hewett while at Brookings, or by Gaddy, and that they have in no way been influenced by Hewett during his service with the U.S. government. The views expressed are his alone and not necessarily those of the U.S. government.

Both authors wish to express their appreciation to Gertrude E. Schroeder for her expert advice and commentary. They also thank the many staff members at Brookings who participated in various phases of the preparation of the book. Andrew Portocarrero played a special role in ensuring the continuity for the project, both through his excellent research assistance to both authors and as coordinator of the technical preparation for publication. Amy Waychoff served as Hewett's research assistant in the initial phase of the project. Michael Levin assisted in research for the manuscript and helped coordinate publication preparations through to the final version. Elisa Barsoum coordinated and processed early stages of the manuscript. Vernon Kelly and Todd Quinn served as verifiers, and interns Kelly Baldrate and Margaret O'Sullivan provided part-time research assistance in the first phase. Vicky Macintyre and Caroline Lalire edited the manuscript; Louise Skillings typed the final version; and Susan L. Woollen prepared it for the typesetter. Florence Robinson provided the index.

Brookings gratefully acknowledges the financial support of the Carnegie Corporation of New York, the John D. and Catherine T. MacArthur Foundation, the Andrew W. Mellon Foundation, and the Tokyo Club Foundation.

The views expressed in this book are those of the authors and should not be ascribed to any of the persons whose assistance is acknowledged above, to the sources of funding support, or to the trustees, officers, or other staff members of the Brookings Institution.

July 1992   BRUCE K. MAC LAURY
Washington, D.C.   *President*

Contents

5. The New Post-Soviet Economies   130

From Shatalin to the Coup *132*
What Kind of Market? *138*
Through Chaos to the Market *144*
Open for Business? *149*
Western Governments and the Post-Soviet Economies *153*

CHAPTER ONE

The Great Experiment in Autarky

AS FUTURE historians look back on the last two decades of the twentieth century they will point to March 1985—the month when Mikhail Gorbachev assumed leadership of the Union of Soviet Socialist Republics—as the watershed at which the former USSR began the painful return from six decades of self-imposed isolation. Gorbachev will receive full credit for initiating the process. But where it will lead, how long it will take to play out, and what Russia and the other nations that once composed the Soviet Union will look like at the end—these are all questions to which there are, as yet, no answers.

For the entire period from Stalin through Chernenko the Soviet system had existed, and in some ways thrived, in virtual isolation from the political, social, and economic systems of the rest of the world. It was a self-imposed isolation, possible only because of the deadly combination of Stalin's ruthlessness and the USSR's great wealth. The ruthlessness destroyed opposition and, for all but a brave few, even the desire to oppose. The riches allowed the USSR to industrialize with almost no outside assistance or finance, except for episodic infusions of technology (in the 1930s, for example). Under the rubric of "socialism in one country" Stalin set out to construct a self-contained system capable of sustaining itself economically, politically, and socially in even the most hostile of external environments.

The result was a system with an enormous appetite for resources

1

and with enormous resources to consume, serving industry and the military first and giving the population job security but few consumer goods. In the thirty years after Stalin's death his successors only fiddled with the system, moderating the political repression somewhat and tinkering with the economy in an effort to ward off the growing forces of inertia that reflected the depletion of the country's material and human resources. By the 1980s Soviet leaders could boast of formidable military power, but at a high and growing cost as the increasingly archaic economic system strained ever more against the increasing weight of diminishing returns and an expanding technological gap with the West.

From the time he assumed power, and even before, Mikhail Gorbachev seemed almost instinctively to understand that Soviet isolation from the world's political and economic systems was a sign of weakness and—ultimately—a deadly threat to the continued survival of the Soviet state. His goal was to end that isolation. He began the process quite successfully with a foreign policy that ended the cold war—winning him the Nobel Peace Prize—and with a set of political reforms that expanded the franchise and greatly increased the accountability of all levels of government. Politically and socially, the USSR began traveling down the long path toward integration into the global community.

In economic matters, however, Gorbachev made much less and much slower progress. Initially, in 1985–86, he and his advisers seemed to believe that a few modest decentralizing reforms in foreign trade decisionmaking—without any accompanying reform of the domestic economy—would be sufficient to begin drawing the Soviet Union into the global economy. No one seemed in that initial period to appreciate the fact that foreign trade performance, far from being independent of the efficiency of the domestic economy, is actually determined by it—or that integration into the world economy could and should be used to drive domestic economic reforms rather than the other way around.

By the end of 1990, a much wiser Gorbachev, by then surrounded by a somewhat different cast of advisers, had come to realize that even for an economy as large and as richly endowed as that of the USSR, integration into the world economy must serve as a vital catalyst for reform. That realization changed the entire tone of the Soviet leaders' discourse as they began to focus on how to create the conditions that would attract foreign investment quickly and in large amounts.

If this conceptual hurdle had been the only impediment to moving ahead, then a strategy might eventually have emerged, both as a result of the increasingly sophisticated internal debate over economic policy and the lessons learned from Eastern Europe's experience in dealing with similar problems, albeit for much smaller, more open economies. But in addition the USSR faced a unique and formidable dilemma in the struggle for autonomy by the multitudinous nationalities within its borders. What began in 1985 as a tame search for a new political and economic system in the USSR became a raucous, chaotic constitutional crisis in which the very legitimacy of central authority was cast into doubt.

Today, in the midst of that revolution, it is still difficult to envision the end point of the process. But enough change has occurred to eliminate some outcomes and to attach probabilities to others. The old Soviet Union of fifteen republics controlled from Moscow has been shoved aside in favor of a system in which a set of independent states, and local units within those new nations, have much more control over their own governance. How much control is still being decided in the parliaments, in ballot boxes, and on the streets. In the new configuration that emerges from the former Soviet Union, the business environment will be at once more open and more chaotic as various authorities vie over who owns what and who has the right to impose what regulations on which economic activities. It is too early to say with any precision how this historic struggle will be resolved. But even now it is possible to begin to piece together a general picture of what the new economic environment will be like: who will make the rules of the game, how stable the financial system will be, how balkanized the market, and so on.

To see where the system seems to be heading, one must first understand where it was when the reforms commenced in the mid-1980s, which is the subject of this chapter. The subsequent three chapters are devoted to the second half of the 1980s and the beginning of the 1990s, the period in which a relatively bold foreign economic policy unfolded against the backdrop of a failed economic reform and an increasingly chaotic economic and political situation. The final chapter analyzes the probable shape of the new economies on the territory of the former USSR and the implications for their interaction with the global economy.

The Soviet Union in the Global Economy

When Mikhail Gorbachev assumed the Soviet leadership in 1985 he found an economy that was big, was inefficient, and was playing a marginal role in the global economy. Each of these characteristics is striking testimony to how far rich resources and ruthless determination can take a country committed to minimizing its links with the outside world.

To put a rough order of magnitude on these three characteristics of the Soviet economy—its size, inefficiency, and marginalization—data for any year in the 1980s would do, since these numbers changed slowly. In this section data for 1985, the eve of Gorbachev's *perestroika*, will be used in order to capture the economy as he saw it when he set out to reform it.

The Size and Efficiency of the Soviet Economy

By world standards the USSR of 1985 was a large economy (table 1-1). The U.S. Central Intelligence Agency (CIA), which provides the only systematic (and well-documented) calculation of Soviet gross national product, estimated that in 1985 Soviet GNP accounted for 15 percent of world GNP, or a little more than half of U.S. GNP. These estimates now have many doubters, and they may be too high. But even if data now unavailable—apparently even to the Soviet State Committee on Statistics and its successor bodies— somehow are found and the figures adjusted, the basic conclusions will not change: this was a very large economy by world standards, but one considerably smaller than that of the United States; and although on a per capita basis Soviet GNP was well above the world

Table 1-1. *The Size of the Soviet Economy, 1985*

Item	World	Soviet Union	Soviet Union as percent of world	United States	European Community	South Korea	China	Japan
1. GNP (billions of 1985 U.S.$)	14,000	2,063	15	3,989	2,250	86[a]	354[c]	1,329
2. Population (millions)	4,889	279	6	239	273	42[a]	1,042[c]	121
3. GNP per capita (1985 U.S.$)	2,863	7,400	258	16,710	8,240	2,020[c]	340[c]	11,010
4. Primary energy consumption (thousand-barrel-a-day oil equivalent)	144,461	25,882	18	35,995	21,092	1,042[c]	10,882[c]	7,516
5. Primary energy production (thousand-barrel-a-day oil equivalent)	122,680[b]	31,085	25	32,677	12,984	n.a.[c]	11,583[c]	1,488
6. Crude oil production (thousand barrels a day)	52,900	11,350	21	8,933	2,928	0[c]	2,496[c]	0
7. Electricity production (billions of kilowatt hours)	9,750	1,544	16	2,635	1,541	n.a.[c]	411[c]	672
8. Crude steel (millions of tons)	698	155	22	80	136	14[c]	47[c]	105
9. Platinum group (thousands of troy ounces)	7,938	3,800	48	n.a.	2.2	0[c]	0[c]	66
10. Automobiles (thousands)	32,310	1,332	4	8,002	10,700	263[c]	n.a.[c]	7,645
11. Grain (millions of metric tons)	1,800	192	11	347	161	7[c]	379[c]	16
12. Meat (millions of metric tons)	151	17	11	26	26	0.6[c]	18[c]	3
13. Railroad freight (ton-kilometers)	7,285	3,718	51	1,288	184	n.a.[c]	813[c]	22

Sources: U.S. Central Intelligence Agency, *Handbook of Economic Statistics, 1986* (September 1986); U.S. Central Intelligence Agency, *Handbook of Economic Statistics, 1988* (September 1988); U.S. Central Intelligence Agency, *Handbook of Economic Statistics, 1990* (September 1990); U. S. Department of the Interior, Bureau of Mines, *Minerals Yearbook, Area Report: International, 1986,* vol. 3; U.S. Department of the Interior, Bureau of Mines, *Minerals Yearbook, Area Report: International, 1985,* vol. 3; Korean Overseas Information Service, *A Handbook of Korea* (1990), pp. 407, 410; John L. Scherer, ed., *China Facts & Figures Annual, 1987,* vol. 10 (Academic International Press, 1988), pp. 10–11, 199; Ichiro Yano, ed., *Nippon: A Chartered Survey of Japan* (1987); and *BP Statistical Review of World Energy,* June 1990.

n.a. Not available.

a. Gross domestic product.

b. Low estimate; includes only major energy-producing countries.

c. Beef, pork, and mutton only.

average, it was considerably below that of the United States, Europe, and Japan.[1]

Disputes over the size of the Soviet economy have always seemed to generate more heat than light, in part because of conceptual confusions, but also because no matter how heated the debate, no new raw data have been generated, and those are what are required to resolve this issue.

The conceptual problems include a tendency to confuse consumer welfare with GNP. Thus travelers to the USSR always seemed unable to resist observing that GNP could not be as high as the statistics said because they could *see* the country was poor. They forgot that they were looking mainly at consumption, which all agreed was *relatively* low in the USSR.

The more general problem was the fixed price system, in which goods in low demand were produced and placed in inventory at full price, hence adding to GNP but not to consumer welfare. In the absence of better inventory data than are now available, it is difficult to adjust for this important phenomenon, even in a back-of-the-envelope fashion. Moreover, as long as markets were prevented from determining prices it was impossible to make the kind of general equilibrium adjustments necessary to estimate the structure and level of Soviet economic activity in world prices.

Soviet strengths by world standards lay in raw materials and in the sheer quantity of capital goods produced. The USSR of 1985 accounted for one-fifth of world crude oil production (making it the world's largest producer of oil), slightly more than one-fifth of world crude steel production, approximately half of the global production of platinum-group metals, and one-tenth of the grain. These are only a few samples

---

1. For a representative argument by one who believes the CIA estimates are too high, see Anders Åslund, "How Small Is Soviet National Income?" in Henry S. Rowen and Charles Wolf, Jr., eds., *The Impoverished Superpower: Perestroika and the Soviet Military Burden* (San Francisco: Institute for Contemporary Studies, 1990), pp. 13–61. The calculations of Åslund and other critics of the CIA estimate are themselves subjected to critical review in Abram Bergson, "The USSR before the Fall: How Poor and Why," *Journal of Economic Perspectives*, vol. 5 (Fall 1991), pp. 29–44.

of a broader set of indicators testifying to the rich resource endowments of the USSR.

Size itself, of course, says nothing about the efficiency with which a system uses its resources.[2] But even a cursory examination of the interrelationship among the rows in table 1-1 provides an indicator, however rough, of the inefficiencies that set the Soviet system apart from the majority of the world's economies, and even from the relatively inefficient United States. For example, while the USSR in 1985 produced $218 of GNP for every barrel of oil equivalent in energy consumption, the United States and the European Community each produced about $300, and Japan almost $500 for every barrel, more than twice the gross energy efficiency of the USSR.[3] Likewise, the USSR produced nearly twice as much steel as the United States, all of which it consumed since it was a net importer of steel and steel products, yet its GNP was roughly half that of the United States. Furthermore, the Soviet Union produced $1.34 in GNP per kilowatt-hour of electricity used (row 1 divided by row 7), well below the output figure for Japan ($2.00), and significantly lower than those for the European Community ($1.62) and the United States ($1.51). None of these comparisons should be taken as more than general orders of magnitude, since differences in efficiency need not be the only explanation for the variations reported here.[4] If Soviet GNP was even lower

2. We have in mind here simply outputs per unit of inputs, what economists call static efficiency. There is an extensive literature on the efficiency of the Soviet economy, but it is almost exclusively devoted to an analysis of dynamic efficiency, that is, the growth of inputs relative to outputs. See, for example, Abram Bergson, "Technical Progress," in Abram Bergson and Herbert S. Levine, eds., *The Soviet Economy Towards the Year 2000* (London: Allen and Unwin, 1983), pp. 34–78.

3. The precise figures (GNP per barrel of oil equivalent) are USSR, $218; United States, $304; European Community, $292; Japan, $484. They are obtained by dividing the first row of figures in table 1-1 by the fourth row (multiplied by 365 days). Given the many caveats involved in GNP estimates for the USSR and foreign GNPs converted at exchange rates into dollars, only the general magnitudes are important. If anything, the Soviet GNP figure here, and therefore the figure for GNP per barrel of oil equivalent, is too high.

4. Some years ago Hewett explored in depth the issue of the apparently high energy consumption in countries belonging to the Council for Mutual Economic Assistance (CMEA), and concluded that, even after accounting for the most important

than the CIA figures used here, then Soviet inefficiency takes on awesome proportions.

Although these high resource utilization rates may reflect some direct wastage, the primary explanation seems to be that so many of the resources were used to produce capital goods that in turn had low productivity. Most telling is the fact that the annual volume of Soviet fixed investment (which in the mid-1980s accounted for nearly a third of GNP) was roughly equal to U.S. investment, with the result that the two nations' underdepreciated capital stocks were about the same size. Yet Soviet GNP was at best only half that of the United States.[5]

To grasp the nature of the inefficiency, consider the case of Soviet tractors. In the early 1980s the USSR produced tractors at a rate of 550,000–580,000 a year—40 percent of world tractor production—of which approximately 350,000 went to agriculture.[6] U.S. farmers purchase 50,000–60,000 tractors a year, which is one-sixth of the

---

potential explanations for variations in energy use (the structure of output, for example), the USSR and Eastern Europe appeared to be inefficient in their use of energy. See Edward A. Hewett, "Alternative Econometric Approaches for Studying the Link between Economic Systems and Economic Outcomes," *Journal of Comparative Economics*, vol. 4 (September 1980), pp. 274–94, esp. pp. 283–93.

5. The investment figures are from CIA, Directorate of Intelligence, *Handbook of Economic Statistics, 1988* (September 1988) p. 32, but Soviet comparisons tell the same story. See *Narodnoe khoziaistvo SSSR v 1988 g.: Statisticheskii ezhegodnik* (National economy of the USSR in 1988: Statistical yearbook) (Moscow: Finansy i statistika, 1989), p. 680. (Hereafter *Narkhoz.*) The Soviet capital stock figure (excluding personal wealth, and presumably with a nominal valuation for land) was R2.33 trillion in 1985 (*Narkhoz*, p. 259), which is $6.15 trillion at the (geometric) mean purchasing power of $2.64 = 1 ruble in the CIA's estimates (CIA, *Handbook of Economic Statistics*, 1988, p. 32). U.S. gross fixed nonresidential private capital—a very rough equivalent to the Soviet figure—was $6.706 trillion in 1985. U.S. Bureau of the Census, *Statistical Abstract of the United States, 1990*, 110th ed. (Department of Commerce, January 1990), p. 536.

6. The 40 percent figure is from David C. Zaslow, "The Modernization of the Soviet Agricultural Machine-Building Industry," CIR Staff Paper 56, U.S. Bureau of the Census, Center for International Research, July 1990, p. 2. Aside from agriculture, tractors are used in the USSR for a wide range of tasks, including road construction, pipelaying, and even road transport—in some cases substituting for work done by trucks in the West. Ibid., p. 1.

Soviet figure.[7] Yet the USSR still had to devote 19 percent of its labor force, or 30 million workers, to agricultural production, and almost three-fourths of those were working manually.[8] The apparent low productivity of tractors (and other agricultural machinery) seems linked to frequent breakdowns and long downtimes, which in turn were due to poor servicing and a shortage of spare parts. Twenty percent to 45 percent of all Soviet tractors were out of service at any one time.[9] Those tractors that were operable were frequently used for inappropriate jobs, owing to the scarcity of specialized farm equipment (particularly pickup trucks), something that significantly reduced their productivity.[10]

Anecdotal information suggests that the tractor situation was representative of most of the Soviet economy. The *quantity* of capital was high, but its *quality* was either relatively low or inappropriate to the uses to which it was put, and servicing was both expensive and ineffective.

Yet anyone familiar with the Soviet economic system knows that its fundamental problem was not simply poorly designed, or poorly manufactured, or poorly serviced equipment. It ran deeper than that. Even perfectly good equipment can stand idle when labor is short, management is incompetent, or spare parts are unavailable because the manufacturer had no interest in making them. The cause of low productivity in the Soviet Union was the system itself, although particular instances of low or zero productivity had many manifestations. But the fact remains that, for whatever combination of reasons, the USSR clearly appeared to be wasting resources, or products heavy in resource content, in comparison with the rest of the industrialized world.

7. Bureau of the Census, *Statistical Abstract*, 1990, p. 654.
8. *Narkhoz, 1988*, pp. 32–33; and Zaslow, "Modernization of the Soviet Agricultural Machine-Building Industry," p. 1.
9. Zaslow, "Modernization of the Soviet Agricultural Machine-Building Industry," p. 1.
10. Zaslow, "Modernization of the Soviet Agricultural Machine-Building Industry," pp. 36, 43.

It was the prospect of reducing that waste by joining the world economy that intrigued Gorbachev and other Soviet leaders. At the same time these macroeconomic indicators of inefficiency reflected inefficiencies in individual factories and farms, and the competition coming with an opening to the world economy would force many of them either to alter their operations dramatically or to close down. Motivated by the fully justified fear of factory closings and unemployment, Soviet leaders were to engage in a basically hopeless search for a way to open the economy without subjecting it to the competition that inevitably accompanies true openness. It is one thing to believe that a country will be better off if it fully internationalizes its productive sector; it is quite another thing to try to find a politically acceptable way to move from virtually total protectionism to that more efficient system.

Sitting on the Margins of the Global Economy

If one judges the Soviet economy of the mid-1980s simply by its connections with the outside world, its mineral wealth is apparent but not its enormous economy. In world financial markets, cross-border investment, or world services, the USSR was insignificant. Most Soviet interactions with the world economy were simple trade, but even there the Soviet share was minimal. Total Soviet exports to the world economy in 1985, even if one includes its trade with socialist countries— itself a significant part of Soviet protectionism—amounted to only $58.2 billion, or 3 percent of world trade.[11] Exports of that size are

11. Official Soviet trade statistics show 1985 exports to socialist countries of R44.3 billion, and to nonsocialist countries of R28.2 billion. *Vneshniaia torgovlia SSSR v 1985 g.: Statisticheskii sbornik* (Foreign trade of the USSR in 1985: Statistical Collection) (Moscow: Finansy i statistika, 1986), p. 8. The figure for trade with nonsocialist countries can be converted at the official rate for that year, $1.20 per ruble, since that is the way Soviet analysts come up with their ruble figures. This yields a dollar value for Soviet exports to nonsocialist destinations of $33.8 billion. (The exchange rate is from "Soviet Foreign Trade Performance in 1985," *PlanEcon Report*, vol. 2 [April 7, 1986], p. 5.)

usually associated with the world's small economies: for example, Belgium-Luxembourg ($53.7 billion in exports in 1985), the Republic of Korea ($30.3 billion), or Hong Kong ($30.2 billion).[12] Moreover, while those countries export significant quantities of sophisticated manufactured goods, the USSR's exports were primarily energy and arms, particularly in the nonsocialist, hard currency market.

As can be seen in table 1-2, 73 percent of the Soviet Union's 1985 exports to nonsocialist countries came from energy (57 percent; oil alone accounting for 44 percent) and arms (16 percent). Although in the late 1980s the share of energy fell somewhat as a result of falling oil prices, the Soviet Union still accounted for 13 percent of world shipments of oil at the end of the decade, and for a much higher 45 percent in gas. This means that the USSR was not a major factor on the oil market, although the Organization of Petroleum Exporting Countries did pay attention in the late 1980s when Soviet authorities said they would move to support OPEC's pricing policies. The gas market is different in that natural gas depends mainly on pipelines for shipment. The Soviet Union accounted for 40 percent of the gas going into the European market.[13]

The only substantial manufactured export of the USSR was weapons, and in 1985 the Soviet Union was the largest arms exporter in the world, accounting for 37 percent of shipments.[14] Some of these

The exports to socialist countries cannot be converted that way. Although that trade is denominated in "transferable rubles" (TRs), which are converted in official statistics at the commercial rate, prices are actually inflated on both exports and imports, and so the de facto exchange rate is considerably below $1.20. To adjust for that, a rate of $0.55 is used, which is close to the Hungarian and Polish cross-rates for the dollar and the ruble that year and which probably accurately reflects the true value of the TR. "Recent Developments in Exchange Rates of the East European Currencies and the Ruble," *PlanEcon Report*, vol. 1 (December 16, 1985), p. 8. At that exchange rate, Soviet exports to socialist countries in 1985 were $24.4 billion (rather than $53.1 billion at the official rate), which yields total exports of $58.2 billion. World exports in 1985 were $1,911 billion. CIA, *Handbook of Economic Statistics*, 1986, p. 22.

12. CIA, *Handbook of Economic Statistics*, 1986, pp. 78–79.

13. *BP Statistical Review of World Energy*, June 1990, pp. 16, 24.

14. Arms Control and Disarmament Agency, *World Military Expenditures and Arms Transfers, 1989* (October 1990), p. 13.

Table 1-2. *Soviet Trade with Nonsocialist Countries, 1980, 1985, 1989*
Billions of current dollars unless otherwise specified

Item	1980		1985		1989	
	Amount	Percent	Amount	Percent	Amount	Percent
	Exports					
Total	35.0	100	33.8	100	42.1	100
Developed West	24.4	70	22.3	66	26.1	62
Developing countries	10.6	30	11.6	34	16.1	38
Machinery and equipment	8.3	24	8.8	26	12.9	31
Arms	5.7	16	5.5	16	8.7	21
Fuels	19.4	55	19.3	57	16.1	38
Oil	15.9	45	14.9	44	12.1	29
Gas	2.9	8	3.9	12	3.0	7
Nonfood raw materials	6.0	17	4.7	14	10.3	24
Metals and minerals	2.0	6	1.8	5	5.7	14
Food	0.5	1	0.5	1	0.8	2
Manufactured consumer goods	0.8	2	0.6	2	0.9	2
Other	0.0	0	0.0	0	1.1	3
	Imports					
Total	32.0	100	32.3	100	43.7	100
Developed West	24.2	76	23.2	72	32.6	75
Developing countries	7.8	24	9.2	28	11.1	25
Machinery and equipment	7.2	23	6.9	21	12.0	27
Fuels	1.4	4	3.5	11	2.1	5
Nonfood raw materials	11.7	37	10.8	33	14.3	33
Metals and minerals	5.2	16	4.5	14	4.9	11
Food	9.8	31	8.5	26	8.7	20
Grain	5.0	16	5.5	17	4.6	11
Other	0.0	0	0.0	0	1.5	3
	Gold, debt, and terms of trade					
Gold sales	1.6	...	1.8	...	3.7	...
Net dollar debt	10.5	...	15.7	...	33.3	...
Nonsocialist oil sales (millions of barrels per day)	n.a.	...	n.a.	...	1.8	...
Nonsocialist terms of trade (1985 = 100)	96	...	100	...	77	...
Nonsocialist export prices	120	...	100	...	98	...
Oil prices	128	...	100	...	64	...
Nonsocialist import prices	125	...	100	...	126	...
Wheat prices	129	...	100	...	125	...

Sources: Export and import data are adapted from *PlanEcon Report*, vol. 6 (May 25, 1990) p. 29. Export and import prices, and terms of trade, are from ibid., p. 6. Gold sales are from CIA, *Handbook of Economic Statistics, 1990*, p. 75. Data on net dollar debt are from ibid., p. 76. Oil export quantities for 1989 are from "Soviet Entry Trade Developments in 1989," *PlanEcon Report*, vol. 6 (June 8, 1990), pp. 4 and 10. The wheat price is for no. 2 hard winter ordinary protein, wheat, f.o.b. Gulf ports, from U.S. Department of Agriculture, *Wheat Situation and Outlook Yearbook* (August 1990), and U.S. Department of Agriculture, *Feed Yearbook* (February 1989). The oil price is for Romashkinskaia 32.4, or Urals Crude (export blend 32), from U.S. Department of Energy, Energy Information Administration, *Weekly Petroleum Status Report*.
n.a. Not available.

exports were for credit, but most were for hard currency or goods salable for hard currency, such as oil.

The Soviet Union's heavy dependence on energy for its export receipts led to large and unpredictable fluctuations in dollar revenues, providing Soviet planners with windfall gains or losses. Over the decade of the 1970s the explosion in oil and gold prices brought the USSR windfall gains of more than $20 billion, essentially "free" imports that planners had not thought they could afford at the beginning of the decade.[15]

In the mid-1980s the pendulum began to swing the other way, almost precisely when Mikhail Gorbachev came into power. Between 1985 and 1989 oil prices fell 40 percent—with virtually all of the decline occurring in 1986—drawing down the average price of all Soviet exports to developed countries by 25 percent. Since import prices were stable (indeed, grain prices even rose somewhat), Soviet terms of trade with nonsocialist countries declined 20 percent during those years. That rapid reduction in the purchasing power of Soviet exports amounted to a windfall loss of approximately $5 billion a year during 1986–89, which Soviet planners had either to absorb by cutting imports, to finance through a combination of gold sales and new borrowing, or to avoid by an increased volume of oil exports. As table 1-2 shows, imports (especially from developed Western countries) were increased rather than decreased during the 1985–89 period. Hence the adjustment to the deterioration in terms of trade came through an increased volume of oil exports (at lower prices) and through gold sales and foreign borrowing. But the weight of the adjustment fell on new debt, since net dollar debt more than doubled.

The experience of the second half of the 1980s provided Soviet leaders, and in particular Mikhail Gorbachev, with an unnecessary reminder of the USSR's precarious position in the global economy. The Soviet Union was essentially a "one-crop" economy, hostage— as all such economies are—to the vagaries of its main exportable

15. Ed A. Hewett, "Foreign Economic Relations," in Bergson and Levine, eds., *The Soviet Economy*, pp. 288–91.

commodity. One of Gorbachev's principal goals was to use his reforms to move the Soviet Union out of the margins and into the mainstream of the global economy, not by increasing the Soviet share of the energy and arms market, but by diversifying into world manufacturing.

The Costs of Isolation

The costs of Soviet economic isolation were readily apparent even to the untrained eye. The typical Soviet consumer of 1985 had only a limited range of goods available, goods that in many cases were antiquated by world standards. A Soviet family relying solely on Soviet-produced goods was, at best, using products typical of the 1950s and 1960s in the developed West. If the trade barriers had not been prohibitive, the world's producers would have found an eager market in the USSR for virtually the entire spectrum of consumer goods, and Soviet producers would either have had to shut down or simply produce for inventory. The same would have been true for producers' goods.

Moreover, many products that were available in the USSR were extremely expensive in relative terms. Simple pocket calculators of the sort sold for $10 or $20 in the United States and even less in Asia cost 50–100 rubles (R) in the USSR, or a quarter to a half of one-month's salary. Color television sets inferior to those selling at the low end of the U.S. market for several hundred dollars, cost about R500—more than two months' wages—in the Soviet Union.[16] Moreover, the quality of these and a myriad of other out-of-date consumer goods, not to mention the after-sales service, was extremely low by the standards of Western industrial countries. Had it not been for protectionism, Soviet producers would have had to either totally revolutionize their production or perish on their own market.

Worse yet, because Soviet planners had consciously tried to max-

16. V. V. Kuznetsov, *Predpriiatie vo vneshneekonomicheskikh sviaziakh* (The enterprise in foreign economic relations) (Moscow, 1990), p. 161; quoted in Phil Hanson, "New Exchange Rate to Govern Ruble for Trade and Investment," *Report on the USSR*, vol. 2 (November 16, 1990), p. 4.

imize industrial concentration within the USSR in an effort to increase their control over the system, they promoted what were in effect monopoly markets. Soviet producers, freed of foreign competition, did not even have to worry about domestic competitors. Most goods were produced by no more than a few manufacturers, and for these producers there were more than enough customers to go around. The result was as close to a pure seller's market as the real world can achieve.

Soviet leaders and planning officials, unable to ignore or explain away the obvious gap between Soviet and global products, were constantly experimenting with ways to induce Soviet producers to raise quality, cut costs, and improve product mix. Much of the history of Soviet planning reforms consisted of attempts to simulate the results automatically achieved through competition without creating a true market and the competition that comes with it. There are an unlimited number of incentive schemes that could have been used to compel producers to meet world standards in their output, and Soviet planners made a serious effort to implement many of them. But, as Soviet enterprises amply demonstrated, there are an unlimited number of ways to subvert these schemes if there is no real threat of competition behind them. As long as a Soviet manufacturer knew that he would face no effective competition either domestically or abroad and that planners would not enforce absolute quality standards, he could, with conviction, devote his time to the serious matter of persuading superiors he was doing all that was humanly possible to meet their unreasonable expectations.

Military hardware is, at first glance, the one area that might appear to throw doubt on this view of protectionism. Even if we adjust for some traditional hyperbole about Soviet weapons systems, clearly the USSR did manage, primarily on the basis of its own technology, to amass a formidable range of modern weapons. The protected economic system seemed able somehow to compete in this area. However, the success of the Soviet military industry came not as a result of protectionism but in spite of it. The weapons industry was precisely the one area in which Soviet planners were subject to competition from the outside. Driven by a desire to match and surpass American weapons, the planners set uncompromisingly high standards for their own arms manufacturers and then enforced those standards by giving military officers direct quality control over weapons design and production. Moreover, many of the usual excuses for poor quality—limited resources, insufficient foreign exchange, recalcitrant suppliers—were undermined by the high priority assigned to military production. The effect was to compel Soviet industry, at whatever cost, to produce weapons that were capable of competing against their Western counterparts. Soviet weapons were therefore reasonably competitive in terms of quality, but they were very costly. In principle, this system could no doubt have obtained the same result in some other limited area, say, household appliances, but at what would have been an enormous cost by world standards.

From the point of view of the world economy, the results of Soviet protectionism were easy to see because the USSR, despite its relatively high level of development in international terms, was unable to compete in manufactured goods markets. Its producers, protected from pressure to keep up with world efficiencies and qualities, fell far behind. Consequently, most Soviet manufactures were difficult, if not impossible, to export. As a result, the Soviet export mix was dominated by raw materials and semiprocessed products. The only manufactured goods— besides arms—that the protected economy could sell tended to be older technologies with generally low profit margins.

The Global Economy in the Soviet Economy

Although the Soviet Union of the mid-1980s was marginal to the global economy, the converse was not true. Despite the efforts of planners to create an economy with minimal links to the outside world, Soviet leaders ended up with an economy that was in significant ways dependent on trade with the global economy. Soviet imports accounted for 14.6 percent of Soviet national income in 1988, or roughly 12 percent of Soviet GNP that year.[17] That is close to the import de-

17. Although Soviet statistics report total foreign trade in rubles, the prices underlying those rubles are a mix of world market prices and bilaterally negotiated intra-

pendence of the United States in recent years, but of course well below that of the smaller countries of Europe.

The sectoral dependence of the Soviet economy on imports varied greatly, as can be seen in table 1-3, which breaks down Soviet imports by the sector to which the products belonged. Imports accounted for 9 percent or more of all sales in the food, light, machine-building, and chemical industries—all critical industries in the Soviet economy.

Even those figures are so highly aggregated that they understate the importance of imports in individual Soviet markets. The general policy of Soviet planners was to use imports in lieu of producing entire groups of products, or at least entire quality ranges of particular products. Competitive imports were regarded as wasteful, the general goal being to produce everything possible and to import only what could not be produced domestically. Although that policy or its effects are hard to document with any precision, they were clearly the main explanation for the high proportion of imports in purchases of the selected product groups shown in table 1-4.

The table suggests that imports dominated the markets for many important products, notably capital goods for the consumer goods and chemical industries as well as selected food categories. Notice also that for a number of these product groups, imports came mainly from socialist countries in 1985, but in succeeding years the Western share increased substantially, particularly in capital goods for consumer goods industries. This reflected an effort under Gorbachev to use Western

---

CMEA prices, meaning that there is no one-to-one relationship between those foreign trade rubles and the domestic ruble. Thus one cannot directly compare Soviet imports in rubles (R69.1 billion in 1985 [*Vneshniaia torgovlia, 1985*, p. 8]) and Soviet national income (R577.7 billion in 1985 [*Narkhoz*, 1985, p. 409]) and be sure the result (12 percent) measures import dependence. Moreover, since national income measures value added only in material sectors, it understates total valued added, probably by something in the order of 25 percent. A better measure can be obtained by converting imports into Soviet domestic prices, which can be directly compared to national income. The 14.6 percent figure is in domestic prices from a recently published Soviet official input-output table. See Vladimir G. Treml, "The Most Recent Input-Output Table: A Milestone in Soviet Statistics," *Soviet Economy*, vol. 5 (October–December 1989), pp. 348, 351. The 12 percent is a rough adjustment that assumes Soviet national income (which excludes most services) is approximately 75 percent of Soviet GNP.

Table 1-3. *Imports and Gross Sales, by Sector, for the Soviet Union in 1988*
Millions of rubles unless otherwise specified

Sector	Gross sales	Imports	Imports/ gross sales (percent)
Electric power	33,319	10	0
Oil and gas	45,604	909	2
Coal	22,016	474	2
Other fuels	735	0	0
Ferrous metallurgy	54,901	3,357	6
Nonferrous metallurgy	34,098	1,501	4
Chemical industry	69,939	7,687	11
Machine building and metal-working	300,800	31,049	10
Timber, wood, paper	44,545	2,346	5
Building materials and glass	37,618	852	2
Light industry	148,899	22,716	15
Food industry	161,873	14,345	9
Construction	165,447	not traded	0
Agriculture and forestry	269,582	8,775	3
Transport and communications	17,684	not traded	0
Other sectors	10,549	1,443	14
Industry not classified elsewhere	32,129	1,168	4
Total	1,449,738	96,632	7

Source: Calculated from Vladimir G. Treml, "The Most Recent Input-Output Table: A Milestone in Soviet Statistics," *Soviet Economy*, vol. 5 (October–December 1989), pp. 348, 351.

technology to upgrade Soviet-produced consumer goods, about which more will be said later.

These data are undeniably fragmentary, yet they strongly suggest that the Soviet economy depended on international trade to a significant degree, despite efforts to minimize the role of foreign trade in the system. More detailed, disaggregated data would no doubt show an even greater dependence.

The Monopoly of Foreign Trade

Stripped to its essentials, the system for managing foreign economic relations that Mikhail Gorbachev inherited in 1985 was the same system used a half-century earlier. Central authorities enjoyed monopoly con-

Table 1-4. *Import Shares of Purchases of Selected Products in the Soviet Union, 1985, 1988, 1989*[a]
Percent

Product	1985	1988	1989
(Metal) rolling equipment	65(38)	53(43)	51(40)
Railroad cranes	23(23)	26(26)	31(31)
Food industry equipment	52(39)	41(29)	39(24)
Textile industry equipment	53(48)	57(46)	58(37)
Dying and finishing equipment	49(35)	69(25)	68(23)
Knitting machines	52(46)	53(39)	68(21)
Equipment for leather, footwear, and fur industries	73(40)	82(18)	82(18)
Chemical industry equipment	56(32)	55(29)	61(20)
Printing industry equipment	56(41)	52(36)	59(29)
Railroad (passenger) cars	25(25)	33(33)	33(33)
Tram cars	35(35)	33(33)	28(28)
Steel pipe	21(3)	18(3)	15(3)
Agricultural pesticides	33(13)	27(12)	27(15)
Wool	24(2)	25(1)	27(1)
Grain	20(2)	16(1)	16(1)
Tea	31(4)	33(7)	35(8)
Sugar	26(23)	25(18)	25(16)
Clothing	24(16)	21(17)	22(17)
Medicines	31(28)	25(23)	28(23)

Source: *Vneshnie ekonomicheskie sviazi SSSR v 1989 g.* (Moscow: Finansy i statistika, 1990), pp. 53–57.
a. The numbers in parentheses are the percentages of total purchases that came from socialist countries.

trol over all but the most minor foreign transactions; they decided on all investments that would affect export potential and import demand; they controlled the disposition of foreign exchange; and they managed the balance of payments (including new debt and gold sales). The system was not designed to sever links between the Soviet and the global economies but rather to control those links from the center, with the intention of making them serve the goals of the plan. Imports were not bad so long as central planners decided what imports in what quantities from what countries. Exports were necessary to pay for imports, but again it was central planners who would decide what to export (or what to attempt to export), when, and to whom.

The institutional details of the system as they evolved over time, or as they existed in 1985, need not be discussed at any length here. By now most of these details are of interest only to those who wish to write a history of Soviet central planning. But an understanding of the basic structure of the foreign trade monopoly and its interaction with the domestic economy is important to set the context for what has happened since 1985. Like all post-Soviet institutions, the systems that today govern foreign economic relations in Russia and the other successor states to the USSR are in transition: they contain elements of the old system combined with elements of a new system in an environment of utter chaos.

The Omnipotent Center

The state monopoly of foreign trade was simply one aspect of the party's monopoly control over all economic transactions in the system. Hence the Politburo of the Communist party of the Soviet Union was the ultimate repository of this monopoly power.[18] Any major decisions regarding foreign economic relations—such as large gold sales, the principles of trade agreements with important countries or with the socialist countries as a whole, or large investment projects involving foreign participation—were all either approved or rejected in the Politburo.

However, as with the remainder of the economy, the details of who would implement the Politburo decisions, and how, rested with the Council of Ministers and its bodies. Within the council the key institution—for the entire economy and for foreign economic relations—was Gosplan (the State Planning Commission). Gosplan would provide the detailed calculations and recommendations used to arrive at Politburo-level decisions, such as those associated with the construction of natural gas pipelines for exporting gas to Europe. Once the go-ahead was given, Gosplan would authorize the investments, allocate the foreign exchange, tell ministries what imports of pipe and com-

18. Unless otherwise indicated, the material in this section is based on Hewett, "Foreign Economic Relations," pp. 291–98; and Ed A. Hewett, "Most-Favored Nation Treatment in Trade under Central Planning," *Slavic Review*, vol. 37 (March 1978), pp. 25–39. Those who are unfamiliar with the basic economic institutions in the domestic economy will find a discussion in Ed A. Hewett, *Reforming the Soviet Economy: Equality versus Efficiency* (Brookings, 1988), chaps. 3, 4.

pressors were allowed, set the targets for gas production and export, and so on. In matters of somewhat lower priority—such as whether to import weaving machines or ready-to-wear clothing—Gosplan would make its decision on the basis of competing claims from various ministries which argued that they needed imports so as to better meet Gosplan's overall production targets.

In this system Gosplan was fulfilling several different functions that are executed more or less automatically by markets in Western countries. Gosplan was a de facto *financial intermediary*, taking tax receipts and surplus capital from enterprise profits and allocating them to investment projects that it thought would best meet plan priorities. Since the ruble was inconvertible, Gosplan carried out a separate financial intermediation that consisted of appropriating the foreign exchange earned through energy, arms, and other exports and allocating it to imports of products.

Gosplan also acted as the ultimate *owner and manager* of productive assets—deciding how they should be expanded through new investments; what products should be produced, using what technologies; and to what customers they should be sold. Gosplan was also, in effect, the *entrepreneur*, deciding which new technologies should be developed, and even which new industries.

All other economic institutions had strictly limited powers, designed primarily to ensure that they conformed with Gosplan's wishes. The fifty-odd branch ministries sitting on the Council of Ministers supervised all important enterprises in the country, with a parallel system at republic and local levels controlling much of the remainder of the system. The main job of the ministries was to disaggregate, transmit, and enforce Gosplan targets. But that, of course, meant that the ministries became advocates for "their" enterprises during the planning process, arguing for more lenient targets and more generous resource allocations, including more foreign exchange. A minister of light industry, for example, under pressure from Gosplan to expand the output of high-quality, fashionable clothing, would argue for foreign exchange to finance higher-quality looms. And he would have some success, although most of his looms would come from Eastern Europe.

The day-to-day management of foreign trade, including actual export and import transactions, was the job of the Ministry of Foreign Trade. All trade agreements were negotiated under the supervision of the ministry; virtually all trade flowed through one of (by 1985) about seventy foreign trade organizations (FTOs), which together controlled virtually the entire spectrum of export and import transactions for the Soviet Union.[19] The FTOs specialized in particular products, such as imports of grain and other selected agricultural products or the export of automobiles. When the minister of light industry was authorized to import machinery and equipment to build a new plant or modernize an existing one, his staff would have to work with the FTO Raznoeksport to arrange for the negotiations and purchase of the equipment. The foreign supplier might never meet the final user in the USSR, negotiating instead with representatives of the FTO. On the export side, the natural gas produced by the Ministry of the Gas Industry would be sold at domestic prices to Soiuzgazeksport, which would handle the negotiation and realization of the foreign sale. Enterprises in the gas industry might never meet a foreign buyer and would never receive anything but rubles for their sale.

The system for pricing exports and imports was critical to sustaining the monopoly and the protectionism for which it was built. When enterprises authorized to purchase foreign equipment finally managed to arrange the transaction with an FTO, they would pay for the equipment in rubles, at a price reflecting the domestic price for comparable Soviet equipment (or as close to comparable as possible), irrespective of the world market price.[20] In this way the system ensured that world prices did not work their way into the irrational domestic price system and upset Gosplan's control over transactions.

Likewise, an exporter received the domestic price, irrespective of

19. Frank E. Blair, *International Marketing Handbook*, vol. 3, 2d ed. (Detroit: Gale Research Company, 1985), p. 3104.

20. Many imported products did not have counterparts in the USSR. In that case, the general practice seems to have been to derive the domestic price from the import price by using the price in hard currency converted at the official exchange rate. See Philip Hanson, Vlad Kontorovich, and Boris Rumer, *Inflation in the Soviet Investment Complex* (Command Economics Research, Inc., 1989). We are grateful to Philip Hanson for this reference.

the world value of the product. In 1967, for example, Soviet wholesale prices for crude oil were set at R1–R3 per barrel, depending on the producing region. This was $1.22–$3.30 at the exchange rates of that time, which compared favorably with the 1967 price of Mideast light crude of $1.50.[21] Those prices stayed the same throughout the 1970s, however, so when Soviet oil on Western markets was fetching $37 in 1981, Soviet producers were still being paid the equivalent of no more than $3.00 at official exchange rates for their oil.[22] When, in 1982, oil prices were finally changed, the ceiling price was raised to a modest R3.70 per barrel.

The effect here—fully intended—was to isolate domestic producers from any information about the scarcity or abundance of their products on world markets, therefore removing any potential signal to them, for example, that exports should rise relative to domestic sales. In the Soviet system that decision lay with central planners, not with producers responding to signals from a world market.

By the mid-1980s Gosplan had become a large foreign exchange trader cum banker cum investor, handling $35 billion a year. It was Gosplan that accepted, through the ministries, the enterprises' applications for the use of foreign exchange and decided where that foreign exchange should be placed. That monopoly power allowed Gosplan to ignore consumer preferences for imported consumer goods, and even producer preferences for imported capital. It was Gosplan—and ultimately the Politburo— not markets registering consumer demands, that controlled the disposition of the nation's foreign exchange reserves and, for that matter, the nation's capital.

The Foreign Trade Monopoly as a Buffer

This prohibitive protective barrier had its uses in the postwar period, particularly in dampening the effects of fluctuations in the world econ-

---

21. Ed A. Hewett, *Energy, Economics, and Foreign Policy in the Soviet Union* (Brookings, 1984), pp. 134–35.

22. In 1981, $37 was the average delivered price in northwest Europe. U.S. Department of Energy, *Weekly Petroleum Status Report*, January–December 1981 issues (average of figures).

omy. For instance, the surge in world oil prices in the 1970s augmented
state coffers, not those of a few private owners of oil assets, and the
windfall gains were used to finance additional imports without additional debt. Some of those imports were for food that improved Soviet
diets. Thus the windfall gains were shared widely, not just by a relative
few as was the case in many other oil producing countries.

By the same token, when Soviet export receipts fell off in the 1980s
as a result of the decline in oil prices, there was no drop in employment
in Soviet industry. Instead, dollar debt rose while aggregate imports
were maintained, so that the costs of the decline were spread over the
entire society (and placed on the shoulders of future generations).

In effect, then, the foreign trade monopoly was acting as the economic equivalent of a sedative, masking the signals that the economy
should adjust. Of course the cost of using the sedative was the failure
to adjust, and those costs later became painfully apparent. By the end
of 1989 the Soviet Union's hard currency debt was, at best, barely
under control. Meanwhile, Soviet consumers were still awaiting the
revolutions in home appliances, electronics, transportation, health care,
and communications that were already being taken for granted in developed Western countries.

Gorbachev's View of the USSR in the Global Economy

Unlike other recent Soviet leaders, Mikhail Gorbachev was determined from the beginning to end Soviet political and economic isolation
by moving on a broad front to assert the USSR's rightful place as a
full participant in world economic and political events. Even before
he assumed the post of general secretary he clearly felt that the heart
of the matter lay in the Soviet economy, as he indicated in his often-
quoted December 1984 speech delivered only a few months before the
death of his immediate predecessor, Konstantin Chernenko: "Only an
intensive, highly developed economy can guarantee the strengthening
of the position of the country in the international arena, and ensure

that it will properly enter into the new century as a great and prospering power.''[23]

And in foreign policy, particularly in the area of arms control and relations with Eastern Europe, Gorbachev showed an audacity that irrevocably changed the global landscape and the world's view of the USSR. In foreign affairs, Gorbachev seemed to know his own mind early on. He had a strategic vision, and he acted boldly to implement it, in many cases clearly moving well ahead of the Soviet foreign affairs bureaucracy. He moved so quickly and decisively that the bureaucracy barely had time to absorb, let alone oppose, one move before another followed.

Economic affairs were a different story. In domestic economic reform Gorbachev seemed to have a much less well-defined vision, and he was therefore less inclined to run over the bureaucracy. On the contrary, he showed a sensitivity to the bureaucracy's concerns—symbolized by his solicitous tolerance of Prime Minister Nikolai Ryzhkov's cautious approach to economic affairs—which stood in stark contrast to his immense self-confidence in foreign affairs. That lack of clarity on domestic economic affairs permitted the bureaucracy to drag its feet on all important initiatives, leading directly to the chaos and economic deterioration that began to characterize the Soviet economy in 1990.[24]

The Parochial Roots of Soviet Foreign Economic Policy

This generally cautious approach in economic affairs reflected a tendency on the part of Gorbachev and all those around him to think

23. M. S. Gorbachev, "Zhivoe tvorchestvo naroda" (Living creation of the people), in Gorbachev, *Izbrannye rechi i stat'i* (Selected speeches and articles), vol. 2 (Moscow: Politizdat, 1987), p. 86.

24. For a general discussion of the early years of Gorbachev's economic reforms, see Anders Åslund, *Gorbachev's Struggle for Economic Reform: The Soviet Reform Process, 1985–1988* (Cornell University Press, 1989); Padma Desai, *Perestroika in Perspective: The Design and Dilemmas of Soviet Reform* (Princeton University Press, 1989); and Hewett, *Reforming the Soviet Economy*.

simplistically and parochially about the causes of Soviet economic backwardness. In the years 1983–85, when Gorbachev was increasingly involved in Soviet economic affairs under Yuri Andropov, and later under Andropov's successor, Chernenko, he spoke constantly of the need to accelerate innovation, particularly in machine building and metalworking, in order to reduce the gap between Soviet and world technological levels.[25]

But when it came to figuring out how to address that backwardness, Gorbachev's approach was highly traditional: more discipline, new incentive schemes, a new centrally directed capital investment policy focusing on renovating existing plants (rather than building new plants), and better planning. To the extent that he referred to the global economy at all, he was using it solely as a yardstick. The basic notion was that the USSR could catch up to the world economy by working harder at it, in part by exploiting the "human factor."

In the early years of Gorbachev's rule there was no indication that he, or his economic advisers, understood that opening the Soviet economy to the world economy might be the only way to become competitive. No one even hinted that a competitive environment, rather than tougher planners and tighter incentive schemes, would be needed to force enterprises to pull themselves up to world standards.

The Parochialism of Soviet Economists

Such a parochial attitude toward the links between the Soviet and the global economies is not at all surprising, given the low, almost nonexistent, attention Soviet economists had traditionally applied to

25. See, for example, his April 1983 speech, "Leninizm–zhivoe tvorcheskoe uchenie, vernoe rukovodstvo k deistviiu" (Leninism is living creative teaching, the true guide to action), in M. S. Gorbachev, *Izbrannye rechi i stat'i* (Selected speeches and articles), vol. 1 (Moscow: Politizdat, 1987), pp. 382–401; his February 1984 speech, "Zakrepliat' dostignutoe, idti dal'she, povyshat' delovitost'" (To consolidate that which has been attained, to move ahead, and to promote a businesslike approach), in ibid., vol. 2, pp. 5–19; and his February 1985 speech, "Kursom edinstva i splochennosti" (By means of a course of unity and solidarity), in ibid., vol. 2, pp. 117–28.

the role of foreign economic relations in their economic system. They treated foreign trade as a separate and second-rank topic, one dealt with primarily by those interested in trade with particular groups of countries: socialist countries, capitalist countries, and so on. Research in foreign economic relations as a field—similar to the research carried out by Western specialists on international trade and finance—was neither encouraged nor rewarded in the USSR. Virtually all of the USSR's prominent economists had made their reputations by working solely on domestic economic affairs, ignoring without a modicum of concern the role of foreign economic factors in the issues they addressed.[26] Articles on price reforms usually disregarded the importance of exchange rates and world market prices in the design of a price system. Papers bemoaning the lack of competition in the Soviet economy due to the high concentration of industry said nothing about the potential role of imports as a force for disciplining would-be monopolists. In general, the notion that foreign trade might be a vehicle for creating a more competitive environment, and therefore for institutionalizing pressure for better quality and lower production costs, was implicitly dismissed.[27]

There are at least two reasons why Soviet economists suffered from an isolationist mind-set. One is familiar to American economists educated in the 1950s and 1960s. It comes from living in a large, well-endowed economy seemingly immune to the major forces operating in the world economy. There is a strong temptation to believe that international factors play a decidedly secondary role in a well-endowed economy, and indeed that such an economy can afford to stand off

26. Oleg Bogomolov, director of the Institute of International Economic and Political Studies (formerly the Institute for the Study of the World Socialist System), was a notable exception. He and his colleagues had used their knowledge of global economies to write about, and lobby for, a more open Soviet economy. There were others in other institutes, for example in the Institute for World Economy (Rair Simonian, Margarita Maksimova). In general, however, the system treated foreign economic affairs as a marginal specialty.

27. Nikolay Ya. Petrakov, "Prospects for Change in the System of Price Formation, Finance and Credit in the USSR," *Soviet Economy*, vol. 3 (April–June 1987), pp. 135–44; and N. Petrakov, *Demokratizatsiia khoziaistvennogo mekhanizma* (Democratization of the economic management mechanism) (Moscow: Economy, 1988).

somewhat from the rest of the world, reaping the benefits of specialization and trade, while avoiding the sometimes unpredictable effects
of world economic cycles. But the postwar reductions in barriers to
trade and investment—which the United States encouraged and greatly
benefited from—and the growing prosperity that followed from that
liberalization created an interdependent global economy. Even the U.S.
economy, large and powerful as it is, feels the effects of global economic forces—most evident in the impact of the oil crises of the
1970s—as an inevitable cost of the enormous benefits of integration
with the global economy.

The other factor that promoted an isolationist outlook in the Soviet
economics profession, but one that was absent in the United States,
was the political support for this stance. Stalin was isolationist, and
so therefore were the social scientists. In the post-Stalin period tacit
isolationism continued to be government policy, in part as a natural
consequence of the cold war. An economist would have needed extraordinary political courage to defy that policy and argue openly in
favor of integration into the world economy as the only way to achieve
world economic standards in Soviet industry.

While the pressure to adopt a pro-isolationist stand in Soviet economics abated in the post-Stalin period, the legacy remained. Soviet
economists continued to think in isolationist terms, and even by the
end of the 1980s few showed any signs of changing their approach.
During 1990, as the Soviet government, and then other groups, came
forward with plans to reform the economy, foreign economic relations
were still treated as a separate and essentially marginal component of
reform. Even the relatively radical Shatalin Working Group's proposed
500-Day Plan all but ignored foreign economic issues in many of its
central proposals for reforming the system.[28] In 1990, as in 1985 and
1965, discussions of foreign economic relations in any proposal for
economic reforms tended to come in a separate section, written by

---

28. Most notable was the virtually total disconnection between the Shatalin Report's plan to introduce a fully convertible ruble and its plan to fix raw material and
fuel prices in interrepublican negotiations, irrespective of their world market prices.
The Shatalin Report is discussed in chapter 4.

different people who rarely discussed in detail their proposals with those writing the main part of the report.

Because, of necessity, Mikhail Gorbachev relied almost exclusively on Soviet economists for his economic advice, he was talking to professionals trained as economic isolationists. It is no wonder that he himself fell into an isolationist trap.

Mikhail Gorbachev's Neo-isolationism

Although Gorbachev's general outlook was clearly global, as were many of his instincts, his views on the links between the Soviet and the world economies were an exception. Here he was unconsciously isolationist. The roots of that isolationism lay first of all in the Soviet capability to produce world-class ideas, which, however, Soviet industry was unable to implement. In this instance Gorbachev was right. Some of the world's leading technologies—including semiautomatic robots for welding pipeline, continuous-casting aluminum, and processes for squeezing juice from fruit—originated in the USSR, but they were developed in the West.[29]

For Gorbachev the next step was quite logical: part of the problem, he concluded, was that imports from the West tended to dampen innovation in the USSR. This "import plague"—as he and some Soviet economists called it—was leading to excessive reliance on foreign technologies and a downgrading of domestic technology. In his widely quoted 1987 book, Gorbachev contended that in a way the USSR had been naive in the 1970s in overestimating the potential benefits of specialization and trade with the West. As a result, some research programs with direct industrial potential were curtailed. The embargoes and boycotts of the Carter and Reagan years had, Gorbachev observed, provided valuable, but expensive, lessons.[30]

29. John W. Kiser, "What Gap? Which Gap?" *Foreign Policy*, no. 32 (Fall 1978), pp. 90–94.

30. M. S. Gorbachev, *Perestroika i novoe myshlenie dlia nashei strany i dlia vsego mira* (Perestroika and new thinking for our country and for the whole world) (Moscow: Politizdat, 1987), pp. 92–93.

The lesson was quite clear, at least in 1985–86. For national security, foreign policy, and economic reasons, Soviet industry had to pull itself up to world technological levels and could do so without significant help from the West. As Gorbachev told the editors of *Time* in 1985:

> We speak openly about our dissatisfaction with the scientific and technological level of this or that type of product. Yet we are counting on accelerating scientific and technological progress not through "a transfer of technology" from the U.S. to the USSR, but through "transfusions" of the most advanced ideas, discoveries and innovations from Soviet science to Soviet industry and agriculture, through more effective use of our own scientific and technological potential. . . . At the same time, we would naturally not like to forgo those additional advantages that are provided by reciprocal scientific and technological cooperation with other countries, including the U.S.[31]

Out of context one might dismiss this as the necessary bravado of the leader of a proud but economically weak country in need of much assistance. But in the framework of Soviet political culture and the entire mind-set of Soviet economics, this was the understandable position of a Soviet politician making economic policy, and he was serious: the USSR did intend to go it alone.

As subsequent developments were to show, Gorbachev believed also that he had, within his own system, the ideal vehicle for accelerating technological change—the Soviet defense industry. In 1985–86 Gorbachev moved to reshape the planning system that controlled civilian industry by drawing on the personnel and administrative methods of the relatively advanced defense industry. He began by appointing Nikolai Ryzhkov, a man whose reputation had been built in the military industrial sector, as chairman of the USSR Council of Ministers.[32]

31. "An Interview with Gorbachev," *Time*, September 9, 1985, p. 25.

32. After graduating from the Urals Polytechnical Institute in Sverdlovsk (now Ekaterinburg) in 1959, Nikolai Ryzhkov was employed by what would later be called the Uralmash Factory, where he rose to the position of director in 1970–75. Uralmash produces heavy machinery, including machinery and equipment for the military. Ryzh-

Ryzhkov and Gorbachev set out to restructure the Soviet economic administration in the image of the defense industry, most notably by creating a set of superministerial bodies charged with managing the unwieldy civilian industry the way the Military Industrial Commission had coordinated military production.[33] Particularly important was the establishment in 1985 of the Machine-Building Bureau, which was given the task of supervising civilian machine building just as the Military Industrial Commission had successfully supervised the military industry. Ivan Silaev, who had a career in the defense sector, was appointed the new bureau's first head.[34] The State Foreign Economic Commission was another of the superministerial bodies formed in 1986 and given the task of managing foreign economic policy, as explained in more detail in chapter 3.

The appointments of these two men to important posts were only two of many such actions in which Gorbachev drew on the considerable executive talent in the defense industrial complex to guide the technological revolution he hoped to engineer in the civilian industry. The logical conclusion of this borrowing from the military rather than from abroad was the widely publicized effort, beginning in 1989, to convert the defense industry to the production of civilian goods.

But despite these less-than-promising beginnings, the neo side of

---

kov moved to Moscow in 1975 as deputy minister in the Heavy and Transport Machine Building Ministry (which supervised Uralmash), and then in 1979 to the position of first deputy chairman of Gosplan, where he was responsible for heavy and military industry. From 1982 to 1985 he served in the Communist party secretariat as the head of the Economic Department. For details, see Alexander G. Rahr, *A Biographic Directory of 100 Leading Soviet Officials* (Munich: Radio Liberty Research, RFE/ RL, 1989), pp. 153–55.

33. Hewett, *Reforming the Soviet Economy*, pp. 335–39.

34. Ivan Silaev graduated from the Kazan' Aviation Institute in 1954 and spent the next twenty years in an aviation plant in Gorky (now Nizhnii Novgorod), beginning as a foreman and ending up in 1971–74 as plant director. He then served as deputy minister and minister of the Aviation Industry, with a brief interruption as minister of the Machine Tool and Tool Building Industry (a civilian machine-building ministry). In 1985 Gorbachev appointed him deputy chairman of the Council of Ministers and chairman of the Machine-Building Bureau, where he served until Boris Yeltsin appointed him chairman of the Russian Republic's Council of Ministers. For additional details see Rahr, *Biographic Directory*, pp. 175–76.

Gorbachev's neo-isolationism was important. His goal throughout the reforms was not to isolate the USSR but to come out of the isolation through a domestically driven technological revolution, and then—from a position of strength—to integrate with the world economy. He was using isolationist means, to be sure, but the goal was decidedly nonisolationist.

CHAPTER TWO

The Diplomatic Offensive

MIKHAIL GORBACHEV began his reforms of Soviet foreign economic policy with a diplomatic offensive designed to normalize Soviet relations with international economic organizations and therefore with the world economy. No matter how far he intended to go in these reforms, this was the logical place to start. If Soviet enterprises were ever to become truly interested in developing export markets, they would need to deal with a friendly, not a hostile, global economy.

The normalization of relations with the global economy should also be viewed as one component of Gorbachev's general effort to establish the USSR as a full-fledged member of the international community. He seemed to understand that a USSR on the margins would have little part in shaping the economic institutions that would govern the increasingly integrated world economy of the twenty-first century. Thus the drive to join international economic institutions and to normalize economic relations with the West was not only intended to expand exports but also to expand Soviet influence in the global economic and political system.

This period also saw the USSR rapidly shed the commitments it had accumulated over four decades in its relations with Eastern Europe and with developing countries. Normalization in this case meant cutting off the aid and trade agreements through which the USSR had subsidized client states in exchange for real or imagined benefits in national security and international economic relations.

New Faces for a New Policy

Gorbachev's first step toward transforming Soviet foreign policy, including foreign economic policy, was to move strong supporters of his views into positions of authority. Eduard Shevardnadze, a man with no experience in foreign affairs but a pragmatist with strong loyalties to Gorbachev, was appointed minister of foreign affairs in 1985. During his five years in that post, Shevardnadze revolutionized Soviet foreign policy.

Another new face was Alexander Yakovlev, formerly ambassador to Canada and then director of the powerful Institute of the World Economy and International Relations (IMEMO), who was appointed a Communist Party Central Committee secretary in March 1986 and made responsible for, among other things, international affairs. He helped Gorbachev to search out bright younger people capable of implementing the new foreign economic policy.

One of Yakovlev's most notable recruits was Ivan D. Ivanov, a former deputy director of IMEMO, who was moved to the Ministry of Foreign Affairs in July 1986 to head its Department on International Economic Organizations and then to the newly formed State Foreign Economic Commission in the fall. Ivanov played a pivotal role in many of the most important changes under the new foreign economic policy. He helped the Soviet Union to achieve observer status in the General Agreement on Tariffs and Trade (GATT); he conducted the negotiations that led to an economic cooperation agreement with the European Community; he helped design the legislation on joint ventures; and he was responsible for a fairly continuous flow of articles discussing Soviet foreign economic policy. In people such as Ivan Ivanov, Gorbachev and Yakovlev found natural allies who had been in the wings for years waiting for the opportunity to normalize (therefore revolutionize) Soviet foreign economic policy.

Soon after Gorbachev became general secretary, the USSR launched a vigorous effort to expand its ties with the most important economic organizations. The three specific objectives here were membership in the GATT; membership in, or at least a "special relationship" with, the International Monetary Fund and the World Bank; and an agreement on economic cooperation with the European Community. Until the fall of 1986 these efforts were managed in an ad hoc fashion by people such as Ivanov, or through the Ministry of Foreign Affairs. Thereafter primary responsibility fell to the newly formed State Foreign Economic Commission, although the Ministry of Foreign Affairs continued to play a role in foreign economic policy.[1]

Entry into the GATT

Membership, or at least observer status in the GATT, was a first priority for Gorbachev and his advisers for at least three reasons. First, they believed their economic reforms would quickly raise the quality of Soviet manufactured goods to a level competitive on the world market. GATT membership would ensure the removal of barriers to planned Soviet exports of those goods. Second, they realized that the

1. Under Eduard Shevardnadze, Soviet foreign and economic policy were merged much more effectively than ever before. It was the Ministry of Foreign Affairs, for example, that combined the Soviet foreign policy interest in Arab countries with oil export policy, engineering Soviet promises on several occasions to cut oil exports in support of OPEC efforts to shore up world oil prices (Patrick Cockburn and Max Wilkinson, "Soviet Union Agrees to Back OPEC Export Cuts," *Financial Times*, January 23, 1987, p. 38; and James Blitz, "Moscow Plans 5 Percent Cut in Oil Exports to West," *Financial Times*, March 7, 1989, p. 32), and it was most likely the ministry that broke precedent, sending observers to a January 1989 meeting of OPEC and non-OPEC oil producers (Steven Butler, "Soviet Observers to Attend Oil Talks," *Financial Times*, January 18, 1989, p. 36). Likewise, it was Shevardnadze who followed up Mikhail Gorbachev's discussions with Italian Prime Minister Bettino Craxi in May 1985, requesting a revival of the stalled CMEA-EC talks on economic cooperation. Anders Åslund, "The New Soviet Policy towards International Economic Organizations," *World Today*, vol. 44 (February 1988), p. 28.

Subsequently, the Ministry of Foreign Affairs further increased its profile in Soviet foreign economic policy by moving Ernst Obminskii in December 1989 from the State Foreign Economic Commission to the post of deputy foreign minister, where he was to oversee the ministry's considerable interests in foreign economic policy. Obminskii took over from the Foreign Economic Commission (and therefore from Ivanov) some of the major "accounts" in foreign economic affairs, most notably the GATT. Interview material.

new round of GATT-sponsored trade talks—the Uruguay Round—
would have far-reaching implications for the global economy and that
the USSR would clearly benefit from taking an active role in those
talks.[2] Finally, there were even those—although probably not Gorbachev himself—who believed that Soviet membership in the GATT
would speed the reform process by compelling the USSR to comply
with the GATT's staunch insistence on economic openness and competition.[3]

The Gorbachev team realized that full GATT membership might
take time. But in the meantime negotiations with the GATT could
serve as a useful tool for expanding export markets through better and
more comprehensive trade agreements. Such agreements had been
among the GATT's primary functions ever since it emerged in 1947.
After the failure of attempts to create an international trade organization, the GATT instead took the form of a contract agreement (hence
the term "contracting parties") among market economies to promote
world trade, and therefore prosperity, by reducing barriers to trade.[4]
That goal was embodied in the four principles to which all GATT
contracting parties subscribe: (1) to strive to lower trade barriers; (2)
to practice nondiscrimination in trade (the most-favored-nation principle); (3) to ensure that tariff concessions, once given, are not re-
scinded without compensation and are not circumvented through other
forms of protection (such as quantitative barriers); and (4) to settle
trade conflicts by consultation through the use of a set of codified and

2. Ivan D. Ivanov, "The Soviet Union in a Changing Global Economic Setting:
The Prospects for Trade-Oriented Growth," study prepared for United Nations Conference on Trade and Development, ST-TSC-4 (New York, April 25, 1986), p. 26.

3. I. Artemev and S. Stankovskii, "GATT i interesy SSSR" (The GATT and the
interests of the USSR), *Mirovaia ekonomika i mezhdunarodnye otnosheniia* (The world
economy and international relations), no. 8 (August 1989), pp. 34–44. This is an
excellent brief for GATT membership, and an enthusiastic, indeed somewhat rosy,
account of the strengths of the GATT as an organization.

4. For an excellent brief discussion of the history of the GATT, see U.S. Congres-
sional Budget Office (CBO), *The GATT Negotiations and U.S. Trade Policy* (June
1987). A more detailed account can be found in John Jackson, *The World Trading
System: Law and Policy of International Economic Relations* (MIT Press, 1989).

mutually agreed upon rules of conduct for trade.[5] These principles manifestly apply to market economies. In particular, compliance with the first three can be corroborated only in a market economy, where decisions on buying abroad as opposed to buying domestically, and on which foreign supplier to use, are openly reached on the basis of economic criteria that include public tariffs. A centrally planned economy in which trade policy is the outcome of a closed administrative process might be willing to comply with the four principles but—by definition—would have difficulty proving that it had done so.

Following those four principles, the GATT contracting parties have engaged in eight rounds of negotiations since 1947, the result of which has been the massive reductions in trade barriers that fostered a postwar boom in trade and created an integrated global economy.

A Rebuff in August 1986

In August 1986, well before Soviet leaders had demonstrated anything close to a commitment to establish a market economy, the USSR asked the GATT if it could sit as an observer in the Uruguay talks (which were scheduled to begin the following month), with the possibility of later obtaining observer status.[6] Although the GATT contracting parties had rejected a Soviet request for observer status submitted in late 1982, the new Soviet leaders apparently felt it was urgent to try again in order to get in on the beginning of the Uruguay Round.[7] The 1986 request was clearly premature, since no substantial changes had yet been made to transform the Soviet Union into the kind of market economy that would be acceptable to the GATT. Still, the Soviet leaders had grounds for optimism. Even back in 1973, the USSR

5. CBO, *GATT Negotiations*, p. xi.
6. Art Pine, "Soviet Union Asks to Join Round of Gatt Talks," *Wall Street Journal*, August 21, 1986, p. 27; and interview material.
7. William L. Richter, "Soviet Participation in GATT: A Case for Accession," *Journal of International Law and Politics*, vol. 20 (Winter 1988), pp. 478–89; and Jozef M. van Brabant, "Planned Economies in the GATT Framework: The Soviet Case," *Soviet Economy*, vol. 4 (January–March 1988), p. 6.

had been invited to participate in the Tokyo Round—an invitation it chose to ignore.[8]

Persistence Pays Off

The United States was opposed to the Soviet Union's August 1986 request (and remained so until 1990) and effectively vetoed its acceptance.[9] Soviet leaders were not discouraged by the rejection, and they continued to send signals indicating that they wanted to participate in the GATT.[10] At the same time the Soviet government pushed to upgrade relations with a number of other international economic organizations to prove that it did indeed intend to enter the world community.[11]

8. Richter, "Soviet Participation in GATT," pp. 496–97. It was at a U.S. suggestion that the rule for participation in the Tokyo ministerial meeting commencing the Tokyo Round be changed to effectively allow any country, whether developed or not, to participate in the negotiations. This was meant to include the USSR, but the Soviets did not respond. See the comments of Åke Lindén (legal adviser to the director-general, GATT Secretariat), in Margaret Chapman, ed., *USSR Participation in The General Agreement on Tariffs and Trade (GATT)*, Proceedings of the American Committee on U.S.-Soviet Relations (1989), pp. 19–20.

9. At the time official U.S. policy was that the USSR, while engaged in interesting discussions on economic reform, still retained a system "fundamentally incompatible with participation in free-world institutions." Until, and if, a real change of course was evident in the Soviet Union, the U.S. government saw no justification for accepting Soviet applications to join the GATT or other economic institutions devoted to improving economic relations among market economies. *National Security Strategy of the United States* (White House, 1988), p. 13.

10. See, for example, V. Kamentsev, "Problemy vneshneekonomicheskoi deiatel'nosti" (Problems of foreign economic activity), *Kommunist*, no. 15 (October 1987), p. 34. In 1988 a Soviet delegation that included Ivan Ivanov visited GATT headquarters, selected European capitals, and the United States to explore ways in which they might move toward membership.

11. During 1985–87 representatives of the Soviet Union:

—successfully lobbied for participation in some form in meetings of the Pacific Economic Cooperation Council and the Asian Development Bank;

—announced at the UNCTAD (United Nations Conference on Trade and Development) VII meeting in July 1987 that it would join the Common Fund for Commodities;

—informed the United Nations that the USSR would pay the $200 million in arrears on payments due to that organization;

—sent observers to a meeting of OPEC and non-OPEC oil producers, and indicated

Meanwhile, Soviet economists proceeded to explore the nature of the GATT and debated the various avenues the USSR might use to join. One possible precedent had been set by Romania and Poland in the 1970s, which had joined as centrally planned economies but promised to expand imports as a quid pro quo for tariff concessions from the GATT contracting parties.[12] Soviet officials in charge of the push to enter the GATT, particularly Ivan Ivanov, were against such an approach, possibly in part because Poland and Romania received so little in return for the commitments they made. They favored, instead, a straightforward Hungarian-type application as a market economy in the making, with a tariff system as the backbone protecting domestic producers from foreign competition.[13] Ivanov, aware of how long it had taken the Eastern European countries to move from observer status to actual membership, was advocating immediate application for full membership.

In early 1990 the United States and other Western countries dropped their opposition to Soviet observer status in the GATT. The Soviet Union applied in March 1990; the United States publicly announced its support in April; and in May the GATT contracting parties agreed

---

a willingness on several occasions to coordinate Soviet and OPEC oil export policy.

For more details see Åslund, "New Soviet Policy," pp. 28–30; and Ed A. Hewett, "The Foreign Economic Factor in *Perestroika*," *Harriman Institute Forum*, vol. 1 (August 1988), pp. 5–6.

12. Ed A. Hewett, "Most-Favored Nation Treatment in Trade under Central Planning," *Slavic Review*, vol. 37 (March 1978), p. 27.

13. On the "Hungarian strategy," see Ed. A. Hewett, "Most-Favored Nation Treatment," p. 27; and Leah Haus, *Globalizing the GATT: The Soviet Union's Successor States, Eastern Europe, and the International Trading System* (Brookings, 1992). Throughout 1987, in numerous meetings, Ivan Ivanov stated his preference for a regular application to the GATT as a market economy, saying only somewhat in jest that it would be necessary to introduce a system with high tariffs so that the USSR would have something to negotiate away: "We interpret [GATT regulations] the following way: We are not protectionist right now. Let us become protectionist and then, from the higher tariff, let us negotiate." *Journal of US-USSR Trade and Economic Council*, vol. 2 (1987), p. 6. In 1988 during the aforementioned (see note 10) visit to the GATT and selected Western capitals, a Soviet delegation came away confirmed in its conviction that the USSR should apply as a market economy on the strength of the economic reform.

to accept the USSR as one of twenty observers.[14] Although this fell short of Ivanov's "maximalist" goals, it was a considerable achievement in light of the overwhelmingly negative response the Soviet Union had received less than four years before. Indeed the rapidity with which the West, particularly the United States, changed its position on the GATT surprised the Soviet leaders.[15] Although some of the credit for this success goes to the perseverance of Soviet officials, the most important reason for the change in the U.S. position was the emerging evidence in 1990 of an increasingly serious Soviet commitment to creating a market economy.

The USSR and the Bretton Woods Institutions

In May 1944 the forty-four governments that had signed the declaration founding the United Nations came together in Bretton Woods, New Hampshire, at the invitation of the United States, to devise international economic organizations that would bring order to postwar relations among the world's economies. The result was the International Monetary Fund, whose mission has been to promote a stable international financial environment conducive to expanding world trade, and the International Bank for Reconstruction and Development (IBRD, more commonly, the World Bank), whose task has been to promote development, especially in the poorer nations of the world.

The USSR participated in the Bretton Woods negotiations, and the

14. "Soviets Apply to GATT," *Wall Street Journal*, March 12, 1990, p. A6; Walter S. Mossberg, "Bush, Gorbachev Agree on Summit Date; U.S. Makes Concession on GATT Talks," *Wall Street Journal*, April 6, 1990, p. A20; and "Soviets Become Observers in Tariff Trade Agreement," *Wall Street Journal*, May 17, 1990, p. A15. The Soviets were restricted from participating in decisionmaking or settlement of trade disputes, nor were they allowed to participate in the spring 1990 session of the Uruguay Round. Burton Bollag, "Soviet Union Becomes Observer in Trade Body," *New York Times*, May 17, 1990, p. D2.

15. Throughout 1989 Soviet officials were talking of one-to-two years before negotiations would commence with the GATT. One official involved in the effort to enter the GATT said he was flabbergasted at the ease with which his country obtained observer status. Interview material.

articles of agreement for both the IMF and the IBRD were specifically designed to facilitate membership for the USSR as a centrally planned economy. Even though the USSR signed the agreements establishing those two institutions, it chose not to join, despite considerable efforts by the United States and other members throughout 1945–46 to convince it to come in. The Soviets gave many specific reasons for this final decision, but perhaps the most important was the deterioration in overall East-West relations in the early stages of the cold war.[16]

By 1947 the Soviet government had already moved beyond mere passive rejection to active attempts to frustrate the operations of the IMF and the IBRD. As it turned out, international hostility to the USSR was sufficient to erode any broad support for its actions.[17] From that time until the mid-1980s Soviet commentary on the Bretton Woods institutions, primarily the IMF, remained critical, particularly of the IMF's inability to foster low interest rates or to control fluctuating exchange rates.[18]

Soviet authorities viewed the IMF as a U.S.-dominated club of rich countries. They knew that the voting rights they could expect would not allow them to play a role commensurate with their perceived status as a superpower. The data requirements associated with membership (for example, information on balance of payments and gold reserves) seemed onerous to them. And the Eastern European experience demonstrated that joining the IMF meant running the risk of internationally sanctioned interference in Soviet internal economic affairs.

Increasing Interest in the IMF and IBRD under Gorbachev

Although there was no official Soviet policy on IMF or World Bank membership (many high-level economic policymakers did not even

16. Valerie J. Assetto, *The Soviet Bloc in the IMF and the IBRD* (Boulder, Colo.: Westview Press, 1988), chap. 3. The Soviets objected in particular to the data requirements associated with membership, but also to the intrusive nature of IMF studies of member states and the rules for voting.

17. Assetto, *Soviet Bloc*, pp. 65–66.

18. As late as 1987 one could find Soviet officials blaming the IMF for fostering instability in the world economic system. See, for example, Åslund, "New Soviet Policy," pp. 29–30.

know what the organizations stood for), Soviet economists close to the leadership developed a position that combined two contradictory views about membership—one public and one private.[19] Publicly, they espoused the view, which became semiofficial policy, that the USSR would not join the IMF until (1) the dollar had been replaced as an international reserve currency or there was a more stable form of international money, possibly special drawing rights (SDRs) or the European currency unit (ECU); (2) the rules governing decisionmaking in the IMF were democratized, which at a minimum meant that no single country would have the power of veto; and (3) the IMF moved to considerably reduce exchange rate fluctuations within much narrower bands than currently existed.[20]

Meanwhile, more privately, Soviet economists acknowledged that the USSR had no chance of joining the IMF until it could show better progress on economic reform. Consequently, they developed a second and more realistic de facto position: although it made sense to try to enter the GATT in 1986, it made no sense to try for IMF membership while plans for economic reform were vague and plans for ruble convertibility were nonexistent.[21] Since there was no provision for observer status in the IMF charter, it was prudent—so the argument went—to wait until the reforms, including the plans for ruble convertibility, were further along. In the meantime the best course of action was to develop low-level contacts with the IMF, which apparently did occur.[22]

The Soviet approach to the GATT and the IMF presented an interesting paradox. The GATT was, at least nominally, a club for market

19. One Soviet official involved in international economic affairs, when asked in 1988 about the Soviet policy regarding membership in the IMF, groaned at the naïveté of the question, explaining that most of the top-level economic officials had no idea what the IMF did and therefore had given no thought to whether to join that unknown organization. Interview material.

20. Although this was not the official position, it was articulated on many occasions in 1986–87 by Ivan Ivanov to various groups to which he spoke, either in the USSR or the West.

21. Interview material.

22. There was at least one visit in October 1988 to the IMF by a small Soviet delegation. The purpose was apparently exploratory talks, and very little seems to have been accomplished. There were probably other visits in 1988–89.

economies which the USSR obviously would have difficulty joining until its economy was truly on the way to becoming like the others. The IMF and IBRD, in contrast, were allowed by their charter to accept nonmarket economies as members. Yet the Soviets began with the GATT, rather than the IMF.[23] The answer to this paradox may lie in Gorbachev's narrow focus in the beginning on trade promotion, rather than on general reform, as the vehicle for penetrating the world market. Certainly some of his advisers believed it was possible for the Soviet Union to join the GATT as a market economy in the making on the strength of its proposed reforms, even though at that stage reforms may have fallen far short of what would be required to create a true market system.

In Search of IMF and IBRD Membership

By 1989 official Soviet policy on the IMF began to change dramatically in favor of membership. In January of that year Mikhail Gorbachev told a visiting delegation representing the Trilateral Commission:

> We, in the Soviet leadership, are on the road to taking fundamental decisions. But we need understanding and reciprocal measures from the other side. We cannot immediately comply with all the rules for participating in the IMF, the IBRD, etc. Objective conditions dictate that. The West also needs to adapt to such a partner as the USSR.[24]

This was a much softer stand than that taken by Gorbachev's advisers a few years earlier. There were no demands concerning changes in decisionmaking rules, complaints about the role of the dollar, or concern about fluctuating exchange rates. The basic message was that the USSR was ready to join the IMF and the World Bank and that it was asking for flexibility in working out the requirements for doing so.

---

23. The authors are grateful to Philip Hanson for pointing out the paradox.

24. "Vstrecha M. S. Gorbacheva s predstaviteliami 'Trekhstoronnei komissii'" (The meeting of M. S. Gorbachev with representatives of the "Trilateral Commission"), *Pravda,* January 19, 1989, p. 2.

By the end of 1989 that was the general message from all levels in the Soviet leadership. Ernst Obminskii, an economist, was promoted in December 1989 to the position of deputy foreign minister with the explicit task of establishing closer contacts with the GATT, the IMF, and the IBRD.[25] The Ryzhkov government's May 1990 plan for creating a market economy included a call for "convergence" with international economic organizations, including the GATT and the IMF.[26] Foreign Minister Shevardnadze told a visiting IMF delegation in July 1990 that the USSR was ready for IMF membership and that in 1945 the Soviet leadership had been mistaken when it failed to heed its own economists, who called for the country to join the IMF in order to avoid the isolation that would result from a refusal to participate.[27]

This drastic shift in Soviet policy can be attributed to at least two factors, one domestic and one foreign. Domestically, Gorbachev and his team had come to realize that successful reform of the Soviet economy would require a significant and sustained inflow of capital from the West. And that would only come about with the blessing of the IMF. Internationally, Western governments had begun withdrawing their opposition to Soviet membership in international economic institutions in response to the dazzling effects of Soviet political reforms, the liberation of Eastern Europe, the enormous progress in arms control, and the increasingly apparent intention in the USSR to create a market economy.

In January 1990 governments in the East and West agreed in principle to create the European Bank for Reconstruction and Development (EBRD), a World Bank–type institution with a founding capital of $12 billion. By February 1991 the details of the agreement had been

25. Vera Tolz, "The USSR This Week," *Report on the USSR*, vol. 1 (December 22, 1989), p. 36.

26. "Ob ekonomicheskom polozhenii strany i kontseptsii perekhoda k reguliruemoi rynochnoi ekonomike: Doklad Pravitel'stva SSSR na tret'iu sessiiu Verkhovnogo Soveta SSSR" (On the economic situation of the country and the concept of a transition to a regulated market economy: Report of the government of the USSR to the third session of the Supreme Soviet of the USSR), Moscow, May 1990, p. 54.

27. Leyla Boulton, "Moscow Ready to Join IMF after 45 Hostile Years," *Financial Times*, July 30, 1990, p. 2.

worked out, and the EBRD began operating on April 15, 1991.[28] The objective of the EBRD, whose founding members included the Soviet Union and Eastern Europe, was to use its capital to foster private investment in those countries.

By July 1990, at a meeting of the heads of the seven leading industrial powers—the so-called G-7—in Houston, Western governments were discussing how they could actively support Soviet economic reforms. The G-7 summit decided to go ahead with an IMF-led study of the Soviet economy, including the participation of the World Bank, the Organization for Economic Cooperation and Development (OECD), and the EBRD. This study was to focus on the state of the Soviet economy, recommendations for its reform, and suggested criteria for Western economic assistance in the transition to the market.[29]

Although the ostensible purpose of the study was no more than those three goals, clearly it could also serve as a first draft of the kind of in-depth study the IMF requires before considering a membership application. Indeed, when Jean-Michel Camdessus, managing director of the IMF, visited Moscow for three days in late July for talks with Soviet leaders about the G-7 study, their discussions covered the entire set of issues associated with membership, including the possible size of the Soviet quota.[30] The talks apparently focused on a quota in the range of $4–$4.5 billion, which put the USSR out of contention for one of the five seats of the IMF's executive committee.[31]

28. "The European Bank: Awkward Fuss," *The Economist*, February 2, 1991, p. 78; and *RFE/RL Daily Report—USSR*, no. 73 (April 16, 1991), p. 1. The EBRD's initial year of operations fell short of the expectations of many observers: by April 15, 1992, the bank had approved only about twenty projects and committed $620 million to all of Eastern Europe and the former Soviet Union. Nicholas Denton, "East Europeans Attack EBRD for Failing to Meet Their Needs," *Financial Times*, April 15, 1992, p. 13.

29. "Excerpts from Economic Declaration by Chiefs of Seven Industrial Nations," *New York Times*, July 12, 1990, p. A15.

30. On Camdessus's visit, see Peter Riddell, "IMF Leads Moscow Delegation," *Financial Times*, July 27, 1990, p. 4. For a Soviet account of the discussions, see "Nas izuchaiut, my izuchaem" (They study us, we are learning), *Izvestiia*, August 5, 1990, p. 2.

31. "Nas izuchaiut, my izuchaem," which is an interview with Viktor Rakov,

A "Special Association" with the IMF and the IBRD

Although the political climate for Soviet membership in the IMF and the World Bank may have been better by the end of 1990 than ever before, the economic reforms remained stalled. The G-7 study published in December 1990 concluded that, without major reforms, there was no justification for sending large capital flows into the Soviet economy.[32] The question then became whether it might not be possible to have something approaching observer status—even if it did not formally exist—as a prelude to membership. In December 1990 the Bush administration took the initiative in defining such a status, proposing that the IMF enter into a "special association" with the Soviet Union, which would preclude IMF-supplied credits but allow the flow of the sort of technical assistance that would be useful in designing a reform package.[33]

---

chief foreign exchange expert of Gosbank. It is clear from Rakov's interview that this figure was not a guess but rather his inference on the basis of extensive discussions with the IMF delegation. Richard Feinberg, in a useful review of the issues surrounding Soviet membership in the IMF and the World Bank, had concluded that the USSR would probably be eligible for a quota of SDR (special drawing rights) 8.1 billion (approximately $10 billion). Richard E. Feinberg, "The Soviet Union and the Bretton Woods Institutions: Risks and Rewards of Membership," Public Policy Papers, Institute for East-West Security Studies, New York, n.d. The actual quotas of the fifteen former Soviet republics, decided in the spring of 1992, totaled about $6.3 billion, nearly $4 billion of which was for Russia. George Graham and Peter Norman, "CIS 'May Need $20 bn Extra Aid,'" *Financial Times*, April 16, 1992, p. 18.

32. International Monetary Fund, International Bank for Reconstruction and Development, Organization for Economic Co-operation and Development, and the European Bank for Reconstruction and Development, *The Economy of the USSR: A Study Undertaken in Response to a Request by the Houston Summit, Summary and Recommendations* (World Bank, 1990). The full three-volume study was subsequently published as *A Study of the Soviet Economy*. The European Community had undertaken a similar study slightly earlier and reached the same conclusions. See "Stabilization, Liberalization and Devolution: An Assessment of the Economic Situation and Reform Process in the Soviet Union," *European Economy*, no. 45 (December 1990).

33. Andrew Rosenthal, "Bush Lifting 15-year-Old Ban, Approves Loan for Kremlin," *New York Times*, December 13, 1990, pp. A1, A22; and Clyde H. Farnsworth, "U.S. Wins Support for Its Approach on Soviet Economy," *New York Times*, December 14, 1990, p. A1. The U.S. proposal, worked out by U.S. Treasury Secretary Nicholas Brady in consultation with his counterparts in the G-7, called for the IMF

Normalizing Bilateral Economic Relations

In addition to making overtures to international economic organizations during the 1985–90 period, Mikhail Gorbachev also oversaw a revolutionary restructuring of Soviet relations with other countries. Western Europe, particularly the European Community, was the starting point for the revolution. The disengagement with Eastern Europe—whose roots reach well back into the Brezhnev period—was the second step, culminating in the January 1991 switch from de facto barter to trade in dollars in Soviet–Eastern European economic relations. Then came a major revision of Soviet policy on foreign aid, beginning with selected cutbacks and ending, after August 1991, with the virtual termination of all aid.

In the main these measures amounted to various forms of what might be termed "normalization" of Soviet relations with other nations—either in the form of establishing ties where few existed before or in the form of cutting off such ties of dependency as are rarely found in the postcolonial world. The net result was to considerably enhance potential Soviet hard-currency earnings by freeing up the raw materials and fuels hitherto exchanged for Eastern Europe's outmoded manufactured goods.

Wooing the European Community

Soviet leaders had regarded the formation of the European Community in 1957 as a hostile act directed against the countries of the Council for Mutual Economic Assistance (CMEA). From then until the early 1970s Soviet policy disparaged the European Community

---

and the World Bank to establish offices in Moscow and to conduct annual reviews of the Soviet economy, as they do for members. The United States intended that this status would "evolve toward full membership." This rather creative scheme was apparently devised by Secretary Brady to stave off a more radical proposal by President François Mitterrand and Chancellor Helmut Kohl favoring immediate membership for the USSR. Farnsworth, "U.S. Wins Support," p. A1.

(EC), and Soviet leaders showed no inclination to establish any relations at all with the organization.

After the common commercial policy came into effect in the EC in 1972, Soviet leaders realized they had to deal with the Community. Thus in the mid-1970s they tried to negotiate a CMEA-EC umbrella agreement on commercial matters. Those efforts failed primarily because the CMEA insisted that it be recognized as an equal partner of the Community, whereas the Community was unwilling to grant the CMEA (by implication) supranational powers for fear Moscow would misuse those powers.[34] Neither the CMEA nor Community members would budge, and the issue remained unresolved until Gorbachev came to power.

Within a few months of assuming the post of general secretary, Mikhail Gorbachev signaled his desire to establish ties with the European Community.[35] His purpose was not only to pick up where matters had left off a decade earlier but to build a base in Europe for the economic opening that served as the centerpiece of the new foreign economic policy.

The CMEA secretariat followed up immediately with a proposal to reopen the issue of the CMEA-EC treaty. The EC responded by proposing a two-track approach: a general agreement between the Community and the CMEA setting a framework for official relations, and bilateral negotiations on commercial issues between the Community and individual CMEA countries.[36] CMEA officials agreed, and in June

34. The Eastern European members of the CMEA had long fought Soviet efforts to transform it into a supranational body. The EC was worried, not without cause, that if it signed a commercial agreement directly with the CMEA, this would strengthen the hold that the organization, and therefore the USSR, had over commercial policies of the individual Eastern European countries. Edward A. Hewett, "Recent Developments in East-West European Economic Relations and Their Implications for U.S.-East European Economic Relations," *East European Economies Post-Helsinki*, Committee Print, Joint Economic Committee, 95 Cong. 1 sess. (Government Printing Office, 1977) pp. 174–98.

35. In May 1985 Gorbachev discussed the matter with Italian Prime Minister Craxi, following up with a letter from Shevardnadze to the EC. Åslund, "New Soviet Policy," p. 28.

36. Haus, *Globalizing the GATT*, chap 5.

1988 the CMEA and the Community signed a joint declaration in which each side recognized the other.[37] By the fall of 1988 the Community had begun trade talks with many of the Eastern European countries, and it had invited most of the countries to send an ambassador.[38] The Soviet representative, Vladimir Chemiatenkov, presented his credentials in Brussels in March 1989, and by July the USSR and the Community had begun negotiations on a wide-ranging trade and cooperation treaty.[39]

Throughout these negotiations the Soviet side sought to obtain the broadest treaty possible, entailing a massive liberalization in trade flows and economic cooperation in numerous specific sectors: energy, transport, the environment, technical standards, nuclear safety, and science and technology. At first the Community held out for a much looser and more modest arrangement, but it soon accepted the more ambitious Soviet goals.[40] After a series of quick and apparently smooth sessions, USSR and EC negotiators met on December 18, 1989, to sign an agreement calling for (1) the complete elimination by 1995 of quotas in Europe's imports from the USSR, in exchange for greater access to the Soviet market; and (2) exchanges of know-how in a number of areas.[41]

37. Joint Declaration on the establishment of official relations between the European Economic Community and the Council for Mutual Economic Assistance.

38. Tom Dickson, "EC and East Bloc States Take Another Step Closer," *Financial Times*, August 17, 1988, p. 2.

39. For a discussion of Chemiatenkov, see Philip Hanson and Vlad Sobell, "The Changing Relations between the EC and the CMEA," Radio Free Europe Research Background Report 73 (May 3, 1989), p. 4. EC and Soviet officials had already held exploratory talks on a trade and cooperation agreement in November 1988, but the EC negotiators told the Soviets they could not go further until they had a mandate from the EC member states to go ahead. David Buchan, "Moscow, EC End Talks," *Financial Times*, November 5, 1988, p. 2. EC Foreign Affairs Commissioner Frans Andrieson presented draft guidelines for the negotiations to the EC Commission in late May 1989, and they were approved in mid-June. Interview material; and David Buchan, "Way Cleared for EC Trade Talks with Moscow," *Financial Times*, June 13, 1989, p. 2.

40. Buchan, "Way Cleared for EC Trade Talks," p. 2; and Buchan, "Moscow, EC End Talks," p. 2.

41. "Agreement between the European Economic Community and the European

The EC agreement, combined with the bilateral agreements arrived at during 1988–89, amounted to a virtually total normalization, or at least the promise of a total normalization, of Soviet relations with the European Community and its member states. From a foreign policy point of view, this was part of the normalization of relations with Europe. For economic policy, this was one of many steps designed to improve the economic environment for Soviet exporters. In addition it served as a prelude to entry into the GATT, not only because the negotiations normalized relations with some of the GATT's most important members but also because the core of the agreement amounted to the mutual granting of most-favored-nation treatment, which would also be the critical issue in joining the GATT.

Taking Eastern Europe off the Dole

In addition to the rapid expansion of relations with Western Europe, Mikhail Gorbachev's new foreign economic policy also called for the demolition of the Soviet–Eastern European relationship he had inherited from his predecessors. It was already clear in the 1970s that Soviet leaders were becoming uncomfortable with the high subsidies implicit in their trade with their allies, particularly Eastern Europe.[42] Throughout the 1980s the Soviet government restricted energy exports for transferable rubles (the "currency" used to put a nominal value on de facto barter deals in the CMEA) to Eastern Europe and pushed hard for a switch from oil to gas (where production costs were lower and the world market more limited). By the time Gorbachev came to power, Soviet leaders had agreed that the Soviet–Eastern European relationship needed an overhaul that would shift the terms of trade toward those implied by world market prices, a move that heavily favored the USSR.

Atomic Energy Community and the Union of Soviet Socialist Republics on Trade and Commercial Economic Cooperation," *Official Journal of the European Communities*, vol. 33 (March 15, 1990), pp. 3–20.

42. Michael Marrese and Jan Vanous, *Soviet Subsidization of Trade with Eastern Europe: A Soviet Perspective*, Research Series 52 (Berkeley: University of California, Institute of International Studies, 1983).

Mikhail Gorbachev responded to, and shaped, that leadership consensus as he (at first very quietly) set about to engineer a quick economic and political disengagement from Eastern Europe. His laissez-faire policy, the enormous influence in Eastern Europe of *perestroika* and *glasnost'*, and the growing urge among Eastern European populations for their independence, all combined to produce the spectacular events of 1989–90, when Eastern Europe was set free to determine its own course.

. Soon thereafter the short-term costs of Eastern Europe's newly won freedom became apparent. Mikhail Gorbachev signed a decree ordering the Soviet government to change—as of January 1, 1991—all trade with CMEA countries from transferable rubles at negotiated prices to dollars at world market prices.[43] Gorbachev's intention was that fuels and raw materials previously tied to imports of Eastern European manufactured goods would now become available for sale for dollars, which in turn could be put to their best use, whether that was in Eastern Europe, Korea, or Western Europe. At a minimum, the USSR could realistically have expected to realize windfall gains of at least $5 billion in 1991 from the shift to dollar pricing in CMEA trade and as much as triple that within a few more years.[44] This was the effect Mikhail

43. "Ukaz Prezidenta Soiuza Sovetskikh Sotsialisticheskikh Respublik: O vnesenii izmenenii vo vneshneekonomicheskuiu praktiku Sovetskogo Soiuza" (Decree of the president of the Union of Soviet Socialist Republics: On the introduction of changes in the foreign economic practice of the Soviet Union), *Pravda*, July 25, 1990, p. 1.

44. The CMEA price system had evolved over a period of thirty-five years into a complicated bilateral bartering system in which, in somewhat oversimplified terms, Eastern Europe came to purchase Soviet energy and raw materials at prices nominally at or above world market prices (using the official dollar-ruble exchange rate) in exchange for sales of its manufactured goods, also nominally at world market prices. Because those Eastern European exports fell well short of Western-quality standards, Eastern Europe was enjoying a subsidy that (depending on the price of oil) approached $20 billion when the oil price was at its relative peak in the mid-1970s. Vanous and Marrese, *Soviet Subsidization*, p. 49. By 1990 that subsidy was much lower, but still rising along with the price of oil, and was estimated to be in the range of $12–$15 billion. "Soviet Economic Performance during the First Half of 1990," *PlanEcon Report*, vol. 6 (July 13, 1990), p. 4. Assuming an immediate switchover to world market prices and no provision of transition credits to Eastern Europe, the Soviet Union would have regarded that entire $12–$15 billion as a windfall gain (presuming

Gorbachev was looking for when he moved to untie the USSR from commitments that had long outlived their usefulness to the Soviet leadership. In fact, the gains in 1991 proved to be much less than planned, owing in large measure to the unanticipated effects of the partial domestic economic reforms, a subject of later chapters.

The Cutback in Foreign Aid

Along with this decision to cut implicit subsidies to the USSR's CMEA trade partners, there were moves to reduce Soviet aid flows to client states in the rest of the world. Beginning in mid-1989 the Soviet press carried an increasing number of complaints against the high cost of Soviet foreign aid in light of difficulties in the domestic economy.[45] By the end of the year a statement by a Ministry of Foreign Affairs official supporting such a new look signaled unmistakably that the government was rethinkng its entire aid policy.[46] Then, in the same decree announcing the changes in pricing and currencies for Soviet-CMEA trade, Gorbachev called for a new approach to foreign aid that would take into account its burden on the nation.[47] This was clearly in response to growing pressure against foreign aid flows in the midst of an economic crisis. In the summer of 1990 the Shatalin reform program, sensitive to the popular mood, called for a 75 percent cut in all forms of foreign aid as part of a stabilization program for the economy during the first 100 days of a 500-day reform.[48]

---

it could sell the oil and gas Eastern Europe would not buy on world markets). If Eastern European economic activity were to fall off because of an inability to finance the balance-of-trade decline (as proved to be the case), the windfall gain would be less. Hence our floor for a realistic estimate at the time of approximately R5 billion.

45. See, for example, V. Skosyrev, "Ot dogm k realizmu" (From dogma to realism), *Izvestiia*, July 10, 1989, p. 5; and B. Sergeev, "Pomogat', no po sredstvam" (Help, but within one's means), *Argumenty i fakty* (Arguments and facts), no. 27 (July 8–14, 1989), p. 2.

46. RFE/RL, *Report on the USSR*, vol. 14 (December 22, 1989), p. 37.

47. In "Ukaz Prezidenta: O vnesenii izmenenii vo vneshneekonomicheskuiu praktiku," Gorbachev ordered the Council of Ministers to be guided by "a calculation of the real possibilities of our country" in determining aid flows.

48. *Perekhod k rynku: Kontseptsiia i Programma*, Chast' I (Transition to the

Unfinished Business

Dramatic as these developments were, the USSR that entered the year 1991 was still a significant distance from truly "normal" relations with the global economy. U.S.-Soviet economic relations were still affected by restraints imposed during the cold war. That, of course, held significance not only for U.S.-Soviet bilateral relations but also for the broader aspirations of the USSR to assume full status among the world's economic powers in international economic institutions.

The USSR was showing surprisingly little interest in a quick improvement in Soviet-Japanese relations, focusing instead in the short run on a rapprochement with the Republic of Korea.[49] And it appeared that the Soviet-German economic relationship, complicated immensely by German reunification, would take some time to normalize.

Still, tremendous changes had emerged in a mere five years. The Soviet relationship with Eastern Europe—economic and political— was irrevocably changed: in the future it would be economics, not politics, that would dominate that relationship. The same could be said of relations between the USSR and developing countries, particularly those that were Soviet clients.

The Soviet relationship with Western Europe was also different from what it had been five years before, although not drastically different. Soviet exports of manufactured goods were not significantly changed

---

market: The conception and program, part 1) (Moscow: Arkhangel'skoe, August 1990), p. 33.

49. Beginning in 1988, Soviet leaders had moved systematically to improve relations with South Korea, at first working through the Chamber of Commerce and Industry (a supposedly nongovernmental body, which allowed Soviet leaders to deny to their North Korean counterparts that the improvement was diplomatically important). By the end of 1989 relations had improved sufficiently to warrant the opening of consular offices in Seoul and Moscow. "Seoul and Moscow Set Up Partial Ties," *New York Times*, December 9, 1989, p. 3. In June 1990 Mikhail Gorbachev met Roh Tae Woo in San Francisco after the U.S.-Soviet summit in Washington. Jane Gross, "Gorbachev, Ending U.S. Trip, Meets with South Korea Leader; Roh Is Optimistic" *New York Times*, June 5, 1990, p. 1. Finally, in December 1990 Roh Tae Woo visited the USSR for further discussions on commercial, as well as general, relations. *Wall Street Journal*, December 17, 1990, p. A1.

from a year earlier, when the new EC-USSR agreement was signed. EC investment in the USSR, though larger than U.S. or Japanese investment, was extremely modest by world standards. The EC-USSR agreement created an environment more conducive than before to expanding trade and cooperation, but the fact remained that it was the Soviet system itself that had to change before the new opportunities could be exploited.

The Limits to Diplomacy

By the end of 1990 Gorbachev's diplomatic offensive had to be considered successful by any standard. The USSR was far closer than it had been five years earlier to being a full-fledged member of the international economic community, which was a tribute to the hard work of its diplomats and economic leaders. It was not there yet by any means, but it could sit in the gallery at the GATT, and a special place was being jerry-built in the IMF and the IBRD. In view of how little had actually changed for the better in the economic institutions that govern economic activity in the USSR, the progress was remarkable.

The relationship with the European Community was symbolic of the general limits of diplomacy as a tool for integrating the USSR into the global economy. To go much further—for example, to achieve GATT membership or IMF or IBRD membership, or to actually begin developing exports of manufactured goods—would require not diplomacy but reform. The diplomats had done their job, and it was now up to the economic leaders to do theirs. It did no good whatsoever to give Soviet enterprises increased access to European markets if the Soviet economic system provided neither the incentive nor the wherewithal for Soviet enterprises to develop those markets.

Mikhail Gorbachev began to address the economic reform side of the equation only after the diplomacy was under way, as he moved to decentralize foreign trade decisionmaking to individual enterprises in an effort to break open the Soviet economy by breaking down the monopoly on foreign trade.

CHAPTER THREE

Requiem for a Foreign Trade Monopoly

THE MONOPOLY of foreign trade that Mikhail Gorbachev inherited in 1985 was consciously designed to discourage, even prevent, enterprises from deciding what they should export, to whom, and at what price.[1] All of that would be given to them by the plan; their job was to fulfill plans, not to second-guess the planners. Soviet enterprises had neither the incentive nor the means to develop and implement an export strategy for their products.

Nor did the enterprises have compelling reasons to economize on imports. Whereas the state paid for imports in dollars, which could be quite costly to earn, the importing enterprise paid in rubles, which were easy to earn. In fact, since enterprises had their goods allocated to them, imports were really free goods, the main cost being the effort required to lobby the supervising ministry and Gosplan for the right to purchase the product. Once received, the imported good might be used or not, depending on the enterprise management's wishes, since it was already "paid for."

The result was a system capable of exporting fuel and raw materials but not manufactured goods, and a system constantly generating demands for imports well in excess of export earnings. There was no

---

1. The term *enterprises* is used here in a generic sense, to include not only what were typically called state enterprises in the USSR but also the various types of associations of enterprises.

55

balance-of-payments crisis, because Gosplan held tight control over imports: demand was high, but authorized imports stayed within the means of the state.

Gorbachev and his advisers set out to change the system by focusing mainly on the export side of the problem. Thus they needed to find ways to create incentives that would induce enterprises to expand exports of manufactured goods, particularly exports for dollars. They were confident at the beginning that they would achieve quick results; indeed, one of the basic motivations for seeking GATT observer status in 1986 was the notion that by the early 1990s Soviet exports of manufactured goods would be expanding so rapidly that the USSR would need membership in the GATT to reduce barriers to the country's exports. The new measures were also designed to encourage enterprises to economize on foreign exchange, and to use it wisely, but the reforms in this area were modest.

The legalization and promotion of joint ventures served as a second pillar of the new policy. Soviet leaders hoped to be able to attract direct foreign investment by offering foreign partners a share in new ventures and the right to repatriate their share of the profits if and when the ventures generated net export revenues. An interest in special economic zones emerged as a natural extension of the new laws on joint ventures, but nothing of substance came of it, largely because the entire idea became entangled in the issue of republican sovereignty.

These measures, most of which were introduced in 1987, were modest by the standards of the Eastern European experience and— more important—far less bold in conception than the diplomatic of- fensive. Their impact on exports was nil, in part because of their modest scale. But the primary problem was the stalled reform of the domestic economy, which negated any small potential benefits the tentative decentralization might have produced.

Unfortunately, the story does not end there. The half-measures of the partial decentralization, combined with the general increase in chaos in the economy beginning in 1989, led to a balance-of-payments crisis in 1989–90 that has been, possibly mistakenly, attributed to the effects of decentralization. It would appear that here, as in the domestic economy, half-measures that were touted as complete reforms made matters worse and thus undermined support for more radical changes.

Selective Devolution of the Foreign Trade Monopoly

The foreign trade monopoly in operation in 1985 was composed of a set of interlocking institutions designed to insulate enterprises and therefore planners from the world economy. Special bodies known as foreign trade organizations handled all exports and imports, thereby cutting off domestic producers and users from contact with the outside world. Producers and users sold to FTOs, or bought from them, at administratively set domestic prices that had no systematic connection with world prices. A rise in the world price, or even a particularly good price for a single export shipment from the USSR, benefited the Soviet state, and possibly the FTO, but never the actual producer. Since the price was the same, domestic enterprises did not care whether they sold a product to another enterprise or to an FTO.

Moreover, because enterprises could sell whatever they produced (or at least be rewarded for it in the form of bonuses), they generally ignored demands for higher quality or after-sales service that filtered through the FTOs from foreign customers. In any economy firms export because they find it profitable, even if troublesome; in the USSR profitability was irrelevant, and enterprises were not looking for more trouble.

Eastern European economies had a similar system imposed on them by the USSR in the 1950s with disastrous results. For small economies dependent on imports of critical inputs and on exports of manufactured goods for their trade receipts, a system that institutionalizes disdain for foreign customers can be ruinous. Consequently, in the 1960s and 1970s virtually all the Eastern European countries moved toward some variant of a system in which large exporters had the right to engage in direct sales abroad and to keep the receipts (converted at one of a set of multiple exchange rates). So if they made a good deal and got a good price, they, not the state, took the money. Although far from dismantling the foreign trade monopoly, this partial dilution on the export side had some modest positive effects in several countries that tried it.

The Soviet economy was different. Rich deposits of fuels and raw materials provided the foundation for a reliable stream of exports that even the hypercentralized, rigid monopoly of foreign trade could manage well enough. The prevailing view in the 1970s, purveyed in particular by the inflexible minister of foreign trade Nikolai Patolichev, was that the foreign trade monopoly was one of the great accomplishments of Soviet socialism and one that no one should dream of tampering with.[2] In large part because of the windfall gains from the OPEC price changes, Minister Patolichev and his allies prevailed: the institutions governing foreign trade decisionmaking in 1985 were substantially the same as those of a half-century earlier.[3]

Mikhail Gorbachev understood that things had to change if the USSR was to wean itself from increasingly expensive raw material and fuel exports and shift to manufactured goods for the bulk of its receipts. As a complement to the diplomatic offensive, he set out to reform foreign trade decisionmaking in much the same way the Eastern Europeans had done in the two preceding decades. His approach to modernizing the foreign trade monopoly was to spin off to ministries, enterprises, and other bodies those portions better managed from below, while keeping control of its key elements in the center.

The State Foreign Economic Commission

Gorbachev began his decentralization in foreign economic relations, as he did in other parts of the economy, with a recentralization. In

2. Ed A. Hewett, "Foreign Economic Relations," in Abram Bergson and Herbert S. Levine, eds., *The Soviet Economy: Toward the Year 2000* (London: Allen and Unwin, 1983), p. 298.

3. Oleg Bogomolov and his colleagues at the Institute for the Study of the World Socialist System used what they had learned in studying Eastern Europe to lobby in the early 1970s for Eastern European–type reforms in foreign trade decisionmaking, but with little success. Interview material. The modest reform that was introduced in 1976 was debated secretly, and the final decree has never been published. Hewett, "Foreign Economic Relations," p. 298.

this case, it took the form of the new State Foreign Economic Commission of the Council of Ministers of the USSR (Gosudarstvennaia vneshneekonomicheskaia komissiia Soveta Ministrov SSSR; hereafter GVK).[4] Established in August 1986, this new superministerial body— somewhat similar in status to the Machine-Building Bureau headed by Ivan Silaev—was charged with coordinating what had hitherto been a surprisingly uncoordinated foreign economic policy.[5] The GVK was given formal control over all foreign economic policy and over all the institutions involved in one or another aspect of foreign economic policy: the Ministry of Foreign Trade, the State Committee for Foreign Economic Relations (mainly responsible for foreign aid), Intourist, the Foreign Trade Bank, the Main Administration for State Tariff Control, and the various commissions and departments somehow engaged in foreign economic activity. The chairman of the GVK was given the rank of deputy chairman of the Council of Ministers, thus outranking the heads of all the organizations that the GVK supervised. However, this status probably overstated his actual powers, since he had a small staff, and in any event the GVK was truly a commission with a fairly conservative membership.[6] The man chosen to head the organization

4. "O merakh po sovershenstvovaniiu upravleniia vneshneekonomicheskimi sviaziami: Postanovlenie Tsentral'nogo Komiteta KPSS i Soveta Ministrov SSSR" (On measures for the improvement of the management of foreign economic relations: Decree of the Central Committee of the CPSU and the Council of Ministers of the USSR), *Ekonomicheskaia gazeta*, no. 4 (January 1987), pp. 3–4. Although published in January 1987, the decree is dated August 19, 1986; a summary version had been published earlier in "O merakh po korennomu sovershenstvovaniiu vneshneekonomicheskoi deiatel'nosti" (On measures for radical improvement of foreign economic activity), *Sotsialisticheskaia industriia*, September 23, 1986, p. 1.

5. Gorbachev was clearly bothered by the fact the the management of foreign economic relations was spread throughout the system with no apparent central coordination. See, for example, his February 1986 speech to the Twenty-seventh Party Congress: M. S. Gorbachev, "Politicheskii doklad Tsentral'nogo Komiteta KPSS XXVII S"ezdu Kommunisticheskoi Partii Sovetskogo Soiuza" (Political report of the Central Committee of the CPSU to the 27th Congress of the Communist Party of the Soviet Union), in Gorbachev, *Izbrannye rechi i stat'i* (Selected speeches and articles) (Moscow: Politizdat, 1987), vol. 3, p. 208.

6. The membership, in addition to the chairman and two of his deputies, included, for example, the deputy chairmen of Gosplan and Gossnab, the minister of foreign

was Vladimir Kamentsev, then minister of fisheries (a ministry with extensive involvement in foreign economic relations).

The GVK's coordinating task was broadly defined to include control over all forms of foreign trade activity, plans for future developments in foreign trade and cooperation, trade promotion, and the general reform process in foreign economic affairs. Its interests encompassed all foreign economic relations with socialist and capitalist countries, developing and developed.[7]

From its founding in 1986 until its dissolution in the spring of 1991, the GVK played a prominent but far from revolutionary role in guiding the reforms in foreign economic relations. In the process the Ministry of Foreign Trade, a mindlessly conservative organization, was eclipsed and eventually merged with the State Committee of Foreign Economic Relations, forming a new body with a smaller staff called the Ministry of Foreign Economic Relations.[8]

Experiments in Direct Foreign Trade Rights

The decree establishing the GVK simultaneously announced a reorganization of the foreign trading system, which amounted to a sub-

---

trade, and the minister of finance, most of whom were quite conservative at the time the GVK began operation.

7. Aside from "O merakh po korennomu sovershenstvovaniiu," see the interview with Deputy Prime Minister Kamentsev, "Sovershenstvovanie vneshneekonomicheskoi deiatel'nosti" (Improvement of foreign economic activity), Ekonomicheskaia gazeta, no. 3 (January 1987), pp. 6–7. The decree establishing the GVK was accompanied by a separate decree specifically directed toward improving economic cooperation with socialist countries. Much of the decree turned out to have no impact, and it is not discussed here. "O merakh po sovershenstvovaniiu upravleniia ekonomicheskim i nauchno-tekhnicheskim sotrudnichestvom s sotsialisticheskimi stranami: Postanovlenie Tsentral'nogo Komiteta KPSS i Soveta Ministrov SSSR ot 19 avgusta 1986 g'' (On measures for the improvement of the management of economic and scientific-technical cooperation with socialist countries: Decree of the Central Committee of the CPSU and the Council of Ministers of the USSR of August 19, 1986), Ekonomicheskaia gazeta, no. 4 (January 1987), pp. 5–6.

8. There was no formal announcement of the dissolution of the GVK. However, in the new list of ministries published on April 10 (Izvestiia, April 10, 1991, p. 2), the GVK was not listed.

stantial reduction in the power of the Ministry of Foreign Trade, and the first important step in dismantling the foreign trade monopoly. The measures contained two closely related innovations. First, they granted direct foreign trading rights to Soviet enterprises and ministries in relatively strong export-oriented industries. It was an idea already under discussion in the USSR in the 1960s and implemented in Eastern Europe in the 1970s.[9] To begin with, most of the FTOs exporting and importing manufactured goods were broken up, or at least considerably reduced in size, as the various product groups for which they had responsibility were shifted to the major producing ministries. For example, the Mashinoexport FTO, a large exporter of mining equipment, tractors, and heavy transport equipment, was broken up and its product nomenclature divided among ten ministries. The export of tractors, for example, was given over to the Ministry of Tractor and Agricultural Machine Building (Minselkhozmash), which created a new organization—Traktoroeksport—to handle the business.

The second innovation was to grant direct trading rights to seventy enterprises in the manufacturing sector, primarily those that were already strong exporters. For example, the Uralmash Production Association in Sverdlovsk (now Ekaterinburg) assumed responsibility for the export of its excavators, the KamAZ Production Association (Kama Truck Factory) for its trucks, and the Nevskii factory for its compressors.[10] Virtually all these enterprises set up their own foreign trading firms (*vneshnetorgovye firmy*) to handle their trading activities.[11]

These twenty ministries and seventy enterprises or associations with direct foreign trading rights were authorized to retain a fixed proportion of their foreign exchange earnings in special accounts that they could then use—without interference from Gosplan or the Ministry of Foreign Trade—for reequipping the enterprise, for purchasing prototypes,

9. A. Anikeev, "Obnovlenie mekhanizma vneshneekonomicheskoi deiatel'nosti" (The renovation of the mechanism of foreign economic activity), *Voprosy ekonomiki* (Questions of economics), no. 8 (August 1990), p. 22.

10. "Svodnye dannye po organizatsii vneshnetorgovykh firm."

11. I. Faminskii, "Sovremennyi etap reformy upravleniia vneshneekonomicheskimi sviaziami" (The current state of reform of the management of foreign economic relations), *Voprosy ekonomiki*, no. 8 (August 1990), p. 17.

and for other similar purposes.[12] The amount retained could range from 2 percent to 97 percent of foreign exchange earnings on manufactured goods exports, although in practice it rarely exceeded 30 percent.[13] Enterprises were prohibited from using their retained foreign exchange to purchase consumer goods for resale or distribution to the work force, although that restriction was partly lifted in 1989.[14]

This scheme was clearly designed to increase exports of manufactured goods from what were already strong export performers, while keeping control over the rest of the system.[15] The proportion of foreign exchange earnings that could be kept by the enterprise was to be fixed for a five-year period so that the enterprise could plan ahead; the prohibition on purchases of consumer goods was designed to ensure that retained foreign exchange went toward improving the export performance of the enterprise.

The state remained in direct control of all trade in raw materials,

12. Ministries were authorized to tax away up to 10 percent of the retained funds of their enterprises for ministerial use, and local authorities could tax away another 5 percent for their own use.

13. Ivan D. Ivanov, "Perestroika vneshneekonomicheskikh sviazei v SSSR: Pervye itogi i osnovnye problemy" (Restructuring of foreign economic relations in the USSR: first results and basic problems), *Mirovaia ekonomika i mezhdunarodnye otnosheniia* (The world economy and international relations; hereafter *MEiMO*), no. 10 (October 1989), p. 9.

14. A September 1987 decree (see note 19) allowed enterprises to use a portion of their retained transferable rubles for consumer goods, but none of their dollars. A December 1988 decree altered that requirement to allow enterprises to use up to 10 percent of retained foreign exchange for the purchase (and resale to their workers) of consumer goods. Very soon that ceiling was raised to 25 percent to allow enterprises to compensate for the "catastrophic" state of the domestic consumer goods market. Ivan D. Ivanov, "Na vneshnii rynok, mimo lozhnykh orientirov" (To the foreign market, past false landmarks), *EKO*, no. 9 (September 1989), p. 88.

15. Soviet leaders were typically secretive about foreign economic policy, allowing only a minimum of public discussion of the pertinent areas. Even under Mikhail Gorbachev, discussion of foreign economic affairs was slower in developing than discussions in other areas. This secrecy was particularly characteristic of these early reforms, which, like large portions of Gorbachev's domestic reforms, had probably already been under consideration during the brief Andropov and Chernenko interregnums.

fuels, food, and selected parts of the machine-building industry through a set of twenty-five FTOs still under the Ministry of Foreign Trade (later the Ministry of Foreign Economic Relations). By the end of the 1980s those FTOs still accounted for 60 percent of all Soviet foreign trade.[16]

The decree on reorganization of foreign trade also specified that the planning authorities would develop special exchange rates to be used in converting export receipts to rubles for each enterprise or ministry, allowing those entities to include foreign trade results in their receipts and therefore in their bonus-determining performance indicators. The result was a rather extensive system of approximately 4,000 adjustments (termed *coefficients*) to the commercial exchange rate, which produced a crazy-quilt system of multiple exchange rates applying almost exclusively to exported manufactured goods.[17] As with all multiple exchange rate systems, this one tended to eliminate most of the differences between world market and domestic prices and therefore virtually destroyed any incentive for Soviet enterprises to choose the foreign over the domestic market, or vice versa.

An enterprise without direct trading rights that wished to export could go through its ministry's FTO, a republican FTO, or—later— even a local FTO. This overlap brought a small element of competition into a hitherto totally monopolized system. Whichever FTO finally handled the transaction was given a commission.

16. Faminskii, "Sovremennyi etap," p. 19.

17. The "differential foreign exchange coefficients" (*differentsirovannye valiutnye koeffitsienty*) were coefficients that, when multiplied by the official exchange rate, yielded the exchange rate for the particular product. There were separate coefficients for different types of currencies: hard, transferable ruble, clearing. There are varying accounts of how many foreign exchange multipliers were in effect at any one time. The figure of 4,000 used here was given by Ivan Ivanov, who was involved in decisionmaking on the coefficients. Ivanov, "Na vneshnii rynok," p. 86.

The multiple exchange rates were developed only for machine-building and manufactured goods—namely those groups eligible for retention quotas; the rest of the product groups had no special exchange rates calculated. A. Burov, "Podkhody k valiutnomu samofinansirovaniiu" (Approaches to foreign currency self-financing), *Ekonomicheskaia gazeta*, no. 20 (May 1988), p. 16.

A Departure from the Past, but a Timid One

Although Soviet leaders had tinkered with foreign exchange quotas in the late 1970s, there had been no publicity, and the policy was subsequently reversed.[18] The 1986 measures were therefore a considerable departure from the past. But they were a cautious departure, and throughout 1987 the leadership showed no inclination to speed up the process.[19] Even after the GVK had authorized the extension of direct foreign trading rights to additional ministries and enterprises in 1987 and 1988, by the end of 1988 only about 160 of the 46,000 industrial enterprises in the USSR were involved, along with 56 ministries and each of the 15 republics.[20]

Most of those enterprises came from the core of Soviet industry, machine building and metalworking. Here the reforms granted direct foreign trade rights and access to special credits to those 119 enterprises (out of a total for these sectors of 9,800) that accounted for 75 percent of the exports of the machine-building and metalworking complex.[21]

The experiment reportedly did put substantial amounts of currency into the hands of the enterprises enjoying the new rights. In 1988 the 240 entities (enterprises, ministries, republics) with direct foreign trade

18. Anikeev, "Obnovlenie mekhanizma," pp. 23–24.

19. There was some fine-tuning to the August 1986 decree a year later, but with no significant new departures. "O dopolnitel'nykh merakh po sovershenstvovaniiu vneshneekonomicheskoi deiatel'nosti v novykh usloviiakh khoziaistvovaniia" (On additional measures for the improvement of foreign economic activity under the new conditions of management), *Ekonomicheskaia gazeta*, no. 41 (October 1987), pp. 18–19. This was a September 17, 1987, decree that strongly asserted the rights of enterprises to use their retained foreign exchange as they saw fit, as long as it was for equipment and services that would expand exports (no consumer goods imports were allowed with hard currency; some consumer goods imports were allowed with the transferable ruble portion of retentions). The loan provisions for the Foreign Trade Bank were liberalized somewhat, but no mention was made of the amounts of funds available. Finally, the decree authorized enterprises to effectively trade their retained foreign exchange among themselves, or to deposit it in interest-bearing accounts in banks should they not immediately want to use it.

20. "Perestroika vneshnikh ekonomicheskikh sviazei" (The restructuring of foreign economic relations), *Izvestiia TsK KPSS*, no. 7 (July 1989), p. 38.

21. Ivanov, "Perestroika vneshneekonomicheskikh sviazei," p. 13.

rights retained accumulated foreign exchange worth R1.3 billion in convertible currency, 2.5 billion in transferable rubles from trade with the CMEA, and R0.9 billion in clearing currency.[22]

The significance of these retained foreign exchange earnings for exporters is difficult to gauge. The R1.3 billion ($2.1 billion) in convertible currency was the most valuable to the exporters, amounting to almost 15 percent of 1988 exports of manufactured goods to non-socialist countries.[23] But special regulations decreed that the exporters had to wait a year to use their earnings; thus the 1988 earnings were not available until 1989. It is quite possible that even then Gosplan delayed in actually giving back to the exporters the foreign exchange to which they were entitled.[24]

The R2.5 billion in retained earnings in exports to socialist countries accounted for 17.1 percent of exports of manufactured goods to those countries.[25] However, the transferable ruble was an inconvertible cur-

22. Ivanov, "Perestroika vneshneekonomicheskikh sviazei," p. 9.

23. The denominator here is the $14.1 billion exports to nonsocialist countries of machinery, equipment, manufactured consumer goods, weapons, and unclassified (presumably manufactured goods). For all the categories except weapons and unclassified goods, it is clear that retention quotas were used; that is also probably true for weapons and other goods ($9.1 billion), since otherwise the retained foreign exchange comes out too high to be believable, given the fact that the bulk of retention quotas were at or below 30 percent. See, for example, Ivanov, "Na vneshnii rynok," p. 87. For the remaining $25.8 billion in exports to nonsocialist countries—65 percent of total exports, comprising mainly raw materials and fuel—there were no foreign exchange retentions. Data on the commodity composition of exports are taken from "Soviet Foreign Trade Performance in 1989," *PlanEcon Report*, vol. 6 (May 25, 1990), p. 20. An exchange rate of R0.61 = $1 is used to convert the retained convertible currency figure to dollars.

24. All foreign exchange earnings went to the Foreign Trade Bank. Those enterprises with the right to retain a portion of the foreign exchange had to wait until one year after they earned it before they could ask for it, and then they had to request it from the Foreign Trade Bank (whose allocations were de facto controlled by Gosplan). Apparently the growing pressure on the Soviet balance of payments in 1988–89 meant that enterprises had a hard time obtaining the foreign exchange they were entitled to. A. Burov, "Eksport: a khorosh li stimul?" (Exports: a good incentive?), *Ekonomicheskaia gazeta*, no. 32 (August 1988), p. 21.

25. Again, the denominators include only exports of machinery, equipment and arms, and manufactured consumer goods to socialist countries, amounting to R14.6 billion (arms and miscellaneous are R4.9 of that). The other 66 percent of exports—

rency, and actual purchases would require a state-to-state agreement with a particular CMEA country. That was understandably difficult to achieve, and therefore many of these rubles may have turned out to be worthless.[26] The same was presumably true of the R0.9 billion holdings in clearing currency, although the Finnish markka portion of these holdings was presumably worth something.

Whatever the problems with these retentions, they did provide direct access to foreign exchange, in contrast to past practice. They also gave some of the USSR's most active exporters limited experience in direct dealings with their customers.

This cannot, however, be interpreted as an unambiguous loosening of controls over the use of foreign exchange. Bureaucratic roadblocks were no doubt thrown in the way of those enterprises seeking to use the foreign exchange to which they were entitled, and it is almost certain that with the new trade rights came the stipulation that imports by those enterprises heretofore financed out of central funds would now have to be paid for by the enterprises themselves. Furthermore, it is likely that the retention ratios in many cases provided enterprises with less foreign exchange than they had previously received through the allocations from their ministries. This was a pay-as-you-go system that overnight hardened manufacturers' convertible currency budget constraints.

Note, too, that this decentralization had only a marginal impact on the planning bureaucracy's control over imports financed from export receipts. The total amount retained in all three currency groups in 1988 was R4.7 billion, or 7 percent of total export receipts. The other 93 percent—all receipts from exports of fuels and raw materials and the centrally retained portion of receipts from sales of other products—remained in the hands of Gosplan, to be allocated as it saw fit. Gosplan's role as de facto financial intermediary remained intact. The main change was the possibility that those manufacturers interested in

---

R28.2 billion, mostly raw materials and fuels—were not eligible for retention quotas. Data on the commodity composition of exports are taken from "Soviet Foreign Trade Performance in 1989," p. 20.

26. Burov, "Eksport: a khorosh li stimul?"

and able to find new export markets could keep a portion of the resulting receipts.[27]

Extension throughout the Economy

Although Soviet officials were less than fully satisfied with the results of the early experiments, they apparently concluded that they needed to go further, not turn back, in order to stimulate export performance.[28] A new decree issued in December 1988 offered direct trading rights to virtually all producing entities, thus completing the dismantling of the foreign trade monopoly. At the same time this decree, and a subsequent March 1989 decree, outlined a completely new mechanism for regulating foreign economic activity, one designed to be compatible with a regulated market economy.[29] The framework

27. Following a provision of the August 1986 decree, the Foreign Trade Bank did issue R1.5 billion ($2.46 billion) in credits to enterprises in support of their efforts to expand exports. Ivanov, "Perestroika vneshneekonomicheskikh sviazei," p. 9. However, this seems to have been merely one of the ways in which Gosplan managed imports, and not the actions of the Foreign Trade Bank as an independent, commercially oriented decisionmaker.

28. In his evaluation of the 1988 results, Ivan Ivanov complained that the 119 machine-building enterprises that had been singled out for particularly high retention quotas performed abysmally. They had promised to raise almost all their product mix up to world standards, but in fact, by GVK estimates, only 12–14 percent of their exports embodied technology comparable to foreign analogues, while 60 percent of their exports should—by GVK assessments—be discontinued. Further signs of inertia for Ivanov were the fact that the machine-building ministries fulfilled 94 percent of their plan for domestic deliveries but only 60 percent of their plan for exports. Ivanov, "Perestroika vneshneekonomicheskikh sviazei," p. 13.

29. The December 1988 decree was entitled "Postanovlenie soveta ministrov SSSR: O dal'neishem razvitii vneshneekonomicheskoi deiatel'nosti gosudarstvennykh, kooperativnykh i inykh obshchestvennykh predpriiatii, ob''edinenii i organizatsii" (Decree of the Council of Ministers of the USSR: On the further development of the foreign economic activity of state, cooperative, and other public enterprises, associations and organizations), *Ekonomicheskaia gazeta*, no. 51 (December 1988), pp. 17–18. A subsequent decree outlining the details of the expanded decentralization was published in March 1989: "Postanovlenie Soveta Ministrov SSSR ot 7 Marta 1989 g. No 203: O merakh gosudarstvennogo regulirovaniia vneshneekonomicheskoi deiatel'nosti" (Decree of the Council of Ministers of the USSR of March 7, 1989, no.

created by this decree guided foreign economic policy in the USSR until the end, including the procedures for controlling trade flows, the strategy for determining the exchange rates, and the conditions governing foreign investment.

Regulations on Who Could Trade

The December 1988 decree, which came into effect on April 1, 1989, offered direct foreign trading rights to virtually any entity producing something: state enterprises and associations, cooperatives involved in production (but not pure trade), and even republics.[30] Any entity wishing direct trading rights was entitled to register with the Ministry of Foreign Economic Relations and to prove that it produced goods "competitive" on world markets. Nowhere was it specified who would decide, and by what criteria, whether a Soviet producer's goods were competitive, so that part of the law was meaningless.

Entities licensed to conduct foreign trade could lose that privilege if they engaged in unscrupulous competition or in activities damaging to state interests. These regulations reflected a fear that enterprises would use their newly won independence to reap profits by buying Soviet products at artificially low state prices and then selling them abroad for huge profits, or that they might acquire products abroad through barter and sell them domestically for large profits. This fear was not unfounded, given the crazy domestic price system.

But in addition, authorities worried that the newly independent entities would do truly foolish things out of a simple lack of experience. Thus one of the grounds for losing direct foreign trading rights was the exportation or importation of low-quality goods; another was the export of goods with either excessively low or excessively high prices. These were two of many examples in which the tone of the documents

---

203: On measures of state regulation of foreign economic activity), *Ekonomicheskaia gazeta*, no. 13 (March 1989), pp. 21–22.

30. Cooperatives are small, owner-operated businesses, legal in some form in the USSR since 1986. See Ed A. Hewett, *Reforming the Soviet Economy* (Brookings, 1988), pp. 340–42. The regulations concerning who can trade, the registration requirements, and other matters were contained in the March 7, 1989, decree.

announcing the decentralization reflected a reluctance by foreign trade officials to relinquish their micromanagement over the process, which they justified by suggesting that Soviet managers would prove to be either too inexperienced or too immature to be fully trusted.[31]

Administrative Controls over What Could Be Traded

The new decree included various provisions for controlling which goods could move in foreign trade in what quantities. Some exports and imports were simply forbidden for these new entities. The initial list included weapons, precious metals and stones, anything associated with nuclear technologies, and narcotics. Similar restrictions applied to imports.[32] These regulations preserved for the state complete control not only in decisions about whether such products should be traded but also in the actual sale and purchase of these products. Over time the list changed somewhat, along with the concerns of the center. Most notable was a series of decisions in 1989 to severely restrict, and in some cases prohibit, the export of consumer goods in an effort to shore up domestic supplies of increasingly scarce durable goods.[33]

31. Later, to justify their cautious pace of decentralization, Soviet foreign trade officials eagerly pointed to what they regarded as irresponsible decisions by enterprises. The GVK found, for example, that the Kubachinskii Artistic Kombinat exported jewelry to a U.S. firm at one-third the price of what Almaziuvelirtorg—the state FTO—received. They also found that the Ministry of the Radio Industry had paid a Norwegian firm R1.5 billion for 60,000 personal computers, along with software, which the GVK judged to be eleven times the realistic value of the deal. *Ekonomika i zhizn'*, no. 7 (February 1990), p. 23. In reality, both cases are probably examples of perfectly rational behavior in the light of distorted domestic prices and a very weak ruble.

32. The complete list is provided in separate regulations (*polozhenie*) issued with the March 7, 1989, decree. See "Polozhenie o poriadke litsenzirovaniia operatsii vo vneshneekonomicheskikh sviaziakh SSSR" (Regulations on the procedure for licensing operations in foreign economic relations of the USSR), *Ekonomicheskaia gazeta*, no. 13 (March 1989), p. 23.

33. "Soviets to Ban the Export of Goods to Ease Shortages," *Wall Street Journal*, January 3, 1989, p. A9; and "O merakh po regulirovaniiu vyvoza iz SSSR tovarov narodnogo potrebleniia" (On measures for the regulation of exports of consumer goods from the USSR), *Sobranie postanovlenii Pravitelstva Soiuza Sovetskikh Sotsialisti-*

The bulk of Soviet foreign trade remained untouched by these restrictions, and to control those flows the regulations introduced a licensing system heavily tilted toward controlling exports. Licenses were required to trade in a list of products that covered about three-quarters of 1989 exports but only about 6 percent of the value of imports.[34] On the export side, products requiring licenses included fuels, raw materials, those metals and stones whose export was not forbidden, some manufactured goods, and selected food and medical products.[35] The list of imports requiring licenses was limited to some medical and chemical products and a few other products. Apparently, controls on imports were to be implemented either through other regulations (for example, direct limits on how enterprises could spend their money) or through foreign trade plans for the direct use of the 90 percent or more of foreign exchange still under direct state control. Although the list of products requiring licenses was issued by the GVK, the actual license decisions were delegated to the bodies directly responsible for the product: the Ministry of Foreign Economic Relations for fuels and raw materials, the Ministry of the Chemical Industry for chemical products, and so on.

The licensing system served two purposes. First, it sought to ensure that products in short supply on the domestic market or those relatively underpriced by world standards would not get out without the authorities knowing about and approving the transactions. This was a terribly important function, since the disequilibrium price system on the Soviet domestic market provided newly empowered entities with endless opportunities to make money by buying goods at absurdly low state prices and selling them for hard currency, which then translated back into huge ruble profits. But it was also an impossible task for an administrative system, and it is hardly surprising that stories began surfacing of various get-rich schemes that the state caught on to only after the fact.[36]

---

cheskikh Respublik (Collected decrees of the government of the Union of Soviet Socialist Republics), no. 30 (August 30, 1989), pp. 742–43.

34. Ivanov, "Perestroika vneshneekonomicheskikh sviazei," p. 12.

35. "Polozhenie o poriadke litsenzirovaniia operatsii."

36. Ivan Ivanov complained of enterprises exporting new rails as scrap metal, for which presumably they received dollars worth many times the value of the ruble

Second, licenses were used to ensure that exports went to specific countries to meet trade agreement commitments or other needs. But again there is evidence that this also proved to be an impossible task.[37] In addition the state retained a powerful tool in its ability to use state orders (*goszakazy*) to require state enterprises to fulfill certain export commitments.[38]

Finally, there was a general prohibition in the law against pure middleman-type activities, to prevent profiteering based on the enormous differences between domestic and foreign prices. The only cooperatives eligible for direct trading rights were those that actually produced something, and they could trade only in what they produced. Even joint ventures could not engage in middleman activities without the expressed approval of the Ministry of Foreign Economic Relations. Any enterprise that failed to comply with these regulations could have its right to engage in foreign trade revoked.

Economic Influences over What Could Be Traded

By extending direct foreign trade rights to a rapidly increasing segment of Soviet enterprises, the December 1988 decree also extended the right to retain and use foreign exchange. This necessitated the elaboration of a set of economic instruments capable of managing foreign economic relations—tariffs and exchange rates being the most important components.

Although the decree retained the system of multiple exchange rates, the intention was to move away from them as soon as possible. It called for work to begin immediately on preparing for a new (presumably devalued) exchange rate to be introduced January 1, 1991, in

---

amounts they had spent to procure the rails inside the USSR. Ivanov, "Na vneshnii rynok," p. 90.

37. Ivanov complained, for example, that 600,000 tons of coal went out via border trade (trade by FTOs representing border regions), when the Soviet state underfulfilled export contracts for 2 million tons of coal. "Na vneshnii rynok," p. 90.

38. This was already a provision in the September 1987 decree, following on the reforms of June 1987 switching from obligatory plans to state orders. See Hewett, *Reforming the Soviet Economy,* pp. 322–33, esp. p. 329.

tandem (as it should have been) with the scheduled reform in domestic prices. As an interim measure the decree ordered a de facto 50 percent devaluation in the commercial exchange rate against convertible currencies, which foreign trade officials calculated would eliminate the need for most of the coefficients.[39] The December decree also called for work to proceed in parallel on a new tariff system, to be integrated into the reformed price system. The proposals were to be submitted by January 1, 1990, and the actual tariffs were to be in place a year later, presumably along with the new exchange rate. The decree stated explicitly that one purpose of the new system would be to facilitate negotiations with the GATT and the European Community, and the general tone of the subsequent debate about the tariff system took for granted that it should be designed to fully conform to GATT rules.[40]

A New Approach to Foreign Exchange and Exchange Rates

The last major component of the new system outlined in the December 1988 decree was a set of measures designed to move in the direction of partial convertibility for the ruble. The decree instructed various parts of the government under the leadership of the State Bank to come up with a plan for this move by the end of March 1989. The intention seemed to be that partial convertibility would come into effect in January 1991, along with the new exchange rate and the new price system, as part of a package leading to a much more decentralized and flexible way of handling foreign trade.

As an interim measure the decree called for periodic currency auc-

39. Technically, the devaluation was to be handled as a 100 percent "markup" (*nadbavka*) to the ruble rate on convertible currency transactions. The rationale for the 50 percent devaluation was apparently that of differential foreign exchange coefficients that cluster around "2" (that is, two domestic rubles for one valuta ruble), and a 50 percent devaluation would therefore eliminate the need for a large part of the coefficients. Interview material.

40. See, for example, Iu. Samokhin, "Tovarno-denezhnye instrumenty upravleniia vneshneekonomicheskimi sviaziiami (regulirovanie importa)" (Commodity-money instruments of the management of foreign economic relations [regulation of imports]), *Vneshniaia torgovlia*, no. 7 (July 1989), pp. 51–54.

tions organized by Vneshekonombank (the Bank for Foreign Economic Relations, the former Foreign Trade Bank, renamed on January 1, 1988). The main (and generally the only) source of foreign exchange in the auctions was retained foreign exchange that the holders wished to auction. The buyers could be state enterprises or production co-operatives but not joint ventures or private citizens. Vneshekonombank could, if it chose, add its own foreign exchange to expand supply but, as it turned out, apparently did so only rarely.

In addition Vneshekonombank received expanded powers to lend foreign exchange to producers for investments that would expand their export capacity quickly. The loans could be as large as $5 billion, and the total size of the loanable funds were to be specified by Gosplan.

Implementation of the December 1988 Decree: Intentions versus Reality

The purpose of the December 1988 decree was to actually bring about the substantive changes that Soviet diplomats were publicly arguing were already under way as they sought to get the Soviet Union into international economic organizations. If the main provisions were implemented as intended, then a Soviet enterprise would be making decisions on exports and imports essentially free of bureaucratic interference, on the basis of economic calculations that would take into account prices influenced by tariffs and by exchange rates reflecting the forces of supply and demand. With that sort of system, they reasoned, it would be relatively easy to enter the GATT and the IMF.

In the final analysis the decree did achieve a great deal, but it also accomplished much less than intended. In itself that is a decent record, judged against past Soviet reform efforts, particularly in foreign economic affairs. Unfortunately, the implementation of the decree also brought on some unforeseen consequences—most notably a balance-of-payments crisis—whose effects are still being felt today.

Sharp Increase in Foreign Trade Eligibility

The December 1988 decree had an immediate and remarkable impact on the number of Soviet firms and organizations eligible to participate in foreign economic activity. When it took effect on April 1, 1989, approximately 240 entities (enterprises, ministries, republics) enjoyed direct foreign trade rights. Three months later, at the end of June 1989, 4,700 economic entities had already been licensed to engage directly in foreign trade.[41] By January 1991 the number had surpassed 26,000 and was still growing.[42]

This explosion greatly expanded employment in foreign economic activities. Unofficial estimates in early 1990 suggested that foreign economic activities employed 100,000 people, up four or five times from the number so employed in the mid-1980s.[43]

The First Tentative Steps toward a Foreign Exchange Market

In implementing the decree, officials did take a few preliminary steps in the direction of a foreign exchange market and therefore a partially convertible ruble. Foreign exchange auctions began in November 1989, and by mid-1990 they were being held on a regular monthly basis. Table 3-1 summarizes the results of the auctions through the first quarter of 1991.

It was clear from early on that Vneshekonombank was unwilling to bolster the supply side with its own money. As a result, the only significant offers came from those few enterprises willing to sell their retained foreign exchange, in most cases because they were having financial difficulties.[44] The result was a narrow mar-

41. "Spisok uchastnikov vneshneekonomicheskikh sviazei SSSR" (List of participants in the foreign economic relations of the USSR), *Vneshniaia torgovlia*, no. 6 (June 1989), p. 1.

42. *Ekonomika i zhizn'*, no. 5 (February 1991), p. 13.

43. V. Burmistrov, "Sovremennye problemy vneshneekonomicheskikh sviazei Sovetskogo Soiuza" (Contemporary problems of foreign economic relations of the Soviet Union), *Vneshniaia torgovlia*, no. 2 (February 1990), p. 5.

44. For a brief but interesting account of the mechanics of the auctions and the motivations of participants by the man charged with running the auctions, see A. Potemkin, "Valiutnye auktsiony v SSSR" (Foreign exchange auctions in the USSR), *Vneshniaia torgovlia*, no. 8 (August 1990), pp. 38–40.

Table 3-1. *Foreign Exchange Auctions, 1989–91*

Date	Sellers	Buyers	Amount traded (millions of valuta rubles)[a]	Rate (ruble/ dollar)[b]
1989				
November 3	31	210	8.4	9.1
1990				
January 17	25	68	8.2	10.5
February 21	n.a.	n.a.	9.0	12.6
April 5	21	86	9.6	13.8
May 10	14	142	9.8	16.3
June 22	27	105	6.8	21.1
July 19	27	88	9.0	24.7
August 31	60	37	11.7	23.2
October 9	55	25	8.0	22.6
October 25	54	17	3.9	20.9
November 15	63	27	8.1	20.9
November 30	88	48	10.0	20.9
December 14	80	68	12.8	21.6
1991				
January 8	57	108	10.9	22.8
January 24	101	117	12.4	25.0
February 13	81	156	11.3	29.7
February 28	93	78	8.6	35.1
March 14	50	26	3.5	35.4

Sources: *Ekonomicheskaia gazeta/Ekonomika i zhizn'*, various issues; and *Vneshniaia torgovlia*, no. 8 (1990), p. 38.

n.a. Not available.

a. The official exchange rate is used. For dates after November 15, 1990, the figures have been converted from the commercial rate.

b. Average of individual prices. The early auctions priced each deal individually.

ket in which generally less than VR10 million, or approximately $18 million, changed hands at an exchange rate that rose throughout most of the period.[45]

That rate was almost forty times the official rate at the time, but the enormous difference in the two rates says little of the overvaluation

45. The auction was for "valuta rubles" (VR), a unit of account freely convertible into dollars at the official rate, which in early 1990 was $1.64. Domestic (inconvertible) rubles were the currency of payment for buyers. Hence the price is actually quoted as domestic rubles per one valuta ruble. The implicit rate between the domestic ruble and the dollar is shown in the last column of table 3-1.

of the domestic ruble since the market was so narrow.[46] If Gosplan (through Vneshekonombank) had chosen to enter the market on the supply side, using the auction to distribute some of its foreign exchange by economic rather than administrative means, the rate would have fallen considerably.

In addition to holding the auction, the government began to signal a willingness to devalue exchange rates, although in a rather haphazard way. The preliminary 50 percent devaluation to the ruble-dollar rate did not come off as scheduled on January 1, 1990. When devaluations did come later in 1990 and in 1991, they were introduced in the midst of great confusion about the economic reform and therefore contributed to, rather than ameliorated, that confusion.[47]

As of the fall of 1990 the new tariff system was still not in place, nor had the foreign exchange coefficients been reduced, both of which had been scheduled for January 1, 1990. The problem in both cases seems to have been a delay in the wholesale price revision also originally scheduled for January 1990. Those measures were finally introduced in 1991, but by then the republican-center conflict had created such chaos that their impact has been difficult to gauge.

---

46. For example, on November 15, 1990, the market settled on a value of 38 domestic rubles as the going price for 1 valuta ruble, which was simply a unit of account worth $1.82 on that day. The result is the implied exchange rate of R20.9/ $1 (R38 divided by $1.82). Since, officially, a valuta ruble "buys" $1.82, but on the auction market a ruble bought only $0.05, the implication is an exchange rate 38 times higher than what is suggested by this very narrow market. In other words, it takes 38 domestic rubles to buy 1 valuta ruble's worth of dollars. In the U.S. economy, as in other market economies, it takes 1 dollar to buy 1 dollar's worth of, say, German deutsche marks.

47. On November 1, 1990, the commercial rate was devalued from R0.6 = $1 to R1.8 = $1 as part of a broad reform of the foreign exchange system (discussed in chapter 4). Also important, though not discussed in the December 1988 decree, the tourist rate for the ruble, which is also that which applies to Soviet citizens exchanging their currency legally, was devalued from R0.62 = $1 to R6.26 = $1 on November 1, 1989. "State Bank Announces Convertible Ruble after 1 Nov.," *Tass*, October 25, 1989, in Foreign Broadcast Information Service, *Daily Report: Soviet Union*, October 27, 1989, p. 94. (Hereafter *Daily Report:SU.*)

Joint Ventures

Parallel with the decentralization in foreign trade decisionmaking, the USSR government announced in January 1987 that joint ventures with up to 49 percent foreign participation would be legal on Soviet territory.[48] This change, although part of the general process of foreign trade reform, was in many ways distinct and deserves separate treatment. Because it was of particular interest in the West, it received a great deal of attention, especially in business circles. In the final analysis, however, joint ventures played a small role in Soviet foreign economic activity and therefore are of somewhat less interest here.

Soviet authorities articulated many goals for joint ventures, but the main ones were to acquire technology and management know-how and to develop exports of manufactured goods. For example, the basic rule was that profit repatriation by a joint venture into convertible currency would normally be possible only in the amount by which gross convertible currency receipts of the venture exceeded gross convertible currency expenditures. Joint ventures oriented solely to the domestic market, even for a high-quality product substituting for products that otherwise would have to be imported, could not repatriate profits directly. If it was skillful and lucky, the joint venture might have been able to get its profits out through barter.[49]

---

48. "O poriadke sozdaniia na territorii SSSR i deiatel'nosti sovmestnykh predpriiatii, mezhdunarodnykh ob"edinenii i firm kapitalisticheskikh i razvivaiushchikhsia stran" (On the procedure for the creation on the territory of the USSR, and on the activity, of joint ventures, international associations, and firms of capitalist and developing countries), an extensive summary of which was published under the heading, "V Sovete Ministrov SSSR" (In the Council of Ministers of the USSR), *Pravda*, January 27, 1987, pp. 1–3.

49. It was possible in a few cases to negotiate a special deal, for example, the American Trade Consortium, which created a more flexible profit repatriation scheme accommodating import-substituting joint ventures. But these were exceptions. Louis Kraar, "Top U.S. Companies Move into Russia," *Fortune*, July 31, 1989, pp. 165–70; and interview material.

The 1987 Decree

Under the January 1987 decree, procedures for registering a joint venture were cumbersome, requiring the approval of several bodies in the slow-moving Soviet bureaucracy. Even when approval was successfully negotiated, the actual operation of the venture presented daunting problems. All purchases from, or sales to, the domestic economy had to be handled through an FTO, since the joint venture was not part of the planning system but rather the equivalent of a hard-currency foreign firm operating within Soviet borders. Furthermore, taxes were high—30 percent on profits (which could be forgiven for two years) and 20 percent on any repatriated profits. And the chairman of the board and the general director of the venture had to be Soviet citizens.

These impediments put off many potential investors; only eight joint ventures had been registered by the end of September 1987.[50] In an effort to speed up the process, the government decentralized approval procedures and liberalized tax-forgiveness rules.[51] This had little apparent effect, although it may have served to speed up, or even save, continuing negotiations. By the end of 1988 there were 193 joint ventures registered in the USSR (including those with socialist countries) with a total capitalized value of R827 million, of which R309 million was the foreign partners' share. That meant slightly less than $500 million in direct foreign investment at most, but probably much less, since many of the joint ventures registered in 1988 did not start operating until 1989 or later.

50. Unless otherwise indicated, figures here and below on the numbers of joint venture registrations are from "Soviet Joint Ventures: Developments through the First Quarter of 1990," *PlanEcon Report*, vol. 6 (April 27, 1990), p. 3, which analyzes data contained in a data bank prepared by the All-Union Scientific Research Institute for Foreign Economic Relations of the State Foreign Economic Commission (hereafter JV Data Bank).

51. "O dopolnitel'nykh merakh, po sovershenstvovaniiu vneshneekonomicheskoi deiatel'nosti," pp. 18–19.

The Move to Liberalize under the 1988 Decree

The December 1988 decree, which opened up direct foreign trade rights to virtually all enterprises, also liberalized procedures for establishing and operating joint ventures. In particular, it introduced the possibility of majority foreign ownership (theoretically up to 99 percent) and of foreign directorship. That decree seemed to open the floodgates, since joint venture registrations jumped from an average of fourteen a month in 1988 to ninety a month in 1989.

Disappointing Results

As of April 1, 1990, the Soviet Union had 1,542 registered joint ventures, of which 1,372 were with market economies. Altogether, the ventures with market economies were capitalized at R3.7 billion rubles, of which R1.3 billion ($2.2 billion) was the foreign partners' commitment, making the average foreign share 35 percent. About three-fourths of that $2.2 billion came in the form of machinery and equipment, the remainder being cash. Although this figure represented commitments associated with registered joint ventures, only about 200 of the 1,542 joint ventures were actually operating, which means that some, probably the bulk, of that $2.2 billion in cash and machinery and equipment was committed but not yet actually paid in or in place.

In addition, most of the joint ventures were small. Sixty percent were capitalized at less than R1 million ($1.6 million), another 25 percent at R1–5 million.[52] Soviet officials caught on to the fact that many joint ventures were simply shells, functioning either as unauthorized representatives for Western firms or as hedges against a takeoff in the economy.[53] Soviet enterprises used joint venture agreements to improve their access to foreign exchange. And although Soviet

52. JV Data Bank, pp. 1–2.
53. B. Tuiukin, "Sovmestnye predpriiatiia: nadezhdy i real'naia otdacha" (Joint ventures: hopes and real results), *Pravitel'stvennyi vestnik* (Government herald), no. 5 (January 1990), p. 10.

leaders hoped to develop exports of manufactured products through joint ventures, most such endeavors were in services. Of the 1,542 registered in April 1, 1990, 208 (13.5 percent) were in computer programming, 149 (9.7 percent) in business consulting, and 129 (8.4 percent) in research and development and engineering consulting. There were only 91 joint ventures with machine-building enterprises (5.9 percent of the total).[54]

Soviet leaders knew that, for all the liberalizations in joint venture laws, the two biggest impediments remained untouched: the restrictions on profit repatriation and the lack of progress on general economic reform. The requirements for profit repatriation forced Western partners to export if they were to make profits in dollars. Yet few Western partners saw any point in manufacturing products in the USSR for sale in the West. Thus the registered joint ventures tended to show up in services.

The lack of progress on overall economic reform made it enormously difficult to operate in the Soviet economy, particularly for a manufacturer. Supplies were undependable in terms of both quality and quantity; the bureaucracy was still in control but was in such a state of flux that it was often difficult to discover who precisely was in charge of what; and the price system was so irrational that joint ventures were required to deal in world market prices with the rest of the economy (which of course used the artificial domestic prices), resulting in much more complex negotiations. In the end it all came down to the lack of progress on economic reform, for even the difficulty in repatriating profits was related to the inconvertibility of the ruble, which in turn reflected the lack of serious reforms.

The Modest Impact of the Reforms

Very little good seems to have come out of the foreign trade reforms of the first Gorbachev years. If anything, they may have made matters

54. JV Data Bank, p. 2.

Table 3-2. *Soviet Exports of Manufactured Goods to Nonsocialist Countries, 1985, 1987–89*
Amounts in billions of dollars

		Manufactured goods				
Year	Total exports	Total	Machinery and equipment	Consumer goods	Arms and other	Other
1985						
Amount	33.8	9.2	3.1	0.6	5.5	24.6
Percent	100.0	27.2	9.3	1.7	16.3	72.8
1987						
Amount	37.9	13.7	4.3	1.0	8.5	24.2
Percent	100.0	36.1	11.2	2.6	22.3	63.9
1988						
Amount	39.9	14.1	4.0	1.0	9.1	26.7
Percent	100.0	35.3	10.1	2.5	22.8	64.7
1989						
Amount	42.1	14.7	3.9	0.9	9.8	27.5
Percent	100.0	3.9	9.3	2.1	23.4	65.2

Source: "Soviet Foreign Trade Performance in 1989," *PlanEcon Report*, vol. 6 (May 25, 1990), p. 20.

worse by at least contributing to the balance-of-payments crisis of 1990 and beyond. Although the design of the reforms themselves deserved some of the blame for this dismal record, the main problem was the failure to move ahead on the general systemic reforms.

No Progress in the Exports of Manufactured Goods

It would require a sophisticated analysis to establish with any certainty if the decentralizing measures affected exports of manufactured goods. But a look at the basic data suggests that they had no discernible impact on sales of manufactured products for hard currency (see table 3-2). It is certainly true that in 1987–89 exports of manufactured goods to nonsocialist countries rose above the 1985 level. But the driving force in the increase was weapons, not civilian goods. In fact, the exports of machinery, equipment, and consumer goods fell off during 1987–89, the very period that decentralization was being extended to an ever-increasing number of enterprises.

Admittedly, these data are a crude test, and a more thorough analysis that separated out price and quantity changes might alter the results somewhat. Nevertheless, the basic conclusion seems clear: the decentralization had no significant impact on exports of manufactured goods during the first few years of its implementation.

This is hardly surprising in light of the conservative elements of the reformers' strategy, combined with the obstructionism of the bureaucracy in implementing the reforms. In the first place, the multiple exchange rates were set to eliminate most of the differences between domestic wholesale and world market prices, effectively eliminating the possibility for high profits in exporting manufactured goods.[55] Even after adjustments were made using the coefficients, it was apparently still more profitable to export primary products, or less processed products, than it was to export manufactured goods, since Soviet primary products are enormously underpriced in domestic prices relative to world prices.[56]

Furthermore, the incentive for enterprises to work hard to develop exports was clearly weakened by the way the decree was actually implemented. Not surprisingly, ministries frequently violated the rule that they could tax only 10 percent of the foreign exchange retentions of their enterprises. This probably meant that enterprises that were successful in developing their exports were forced to make a new deal with the ministry to divide up the spoils.[57] For whatever earnings the enterprise actually managed to retain, financial authorities made it difficult to actually get to them because of the country's general balance of payments difficulties.[58]

55. Burov, "Podkhody k valiutnomu samofinansirovaniiu," p. 16.
56. The irrationalities in this price system were enormous. It was twice as profitable to export natural gas as it was to export diesel fuel, and one-and-a-half times as profitable to export timber as to export cellulose. See, for example, the discussion of V. M. Kamentsev before the International Policy Commission of the Central Committee, in "Perestroika vneshnikh ekonomicheskikh sviazei," p. 40.
57. "Vneshnie sviazi sovetskikh predpriiatii" (The foreign relations of Soviet enterprises) (interview with Igor Faminskii), *MEiMO* (January 1990), p. 61.
58. Burov, "Podkhody k valilutnomu samofinansirovaniiu."

The Balance of Payments Crisis of 1990

If the impact of the foreign trade reforms had been confined to unfulfilled expectations for exports of manufactured goods, there would have been little to distinguish these reforms from other, earlier efforts. But in 1989 the decentralization in foreign trade decisionmaking combined with the growing chaos in the system produced a rather severe balance of payments crisis. It began during fall 1989 and continued throughout 1990.

The Nature of the Crisis

The first sign of trouble came in the fall of 1989 when companies exporting to the USSR began to complain that they were not being paid in a timely fashion. These were virtually all supplier credits, many of them with companies that had dealt with the USSR for decades without even a hint of trouble. Vneshekonombank continued to service debt it had incurred, even into 1991.[59] By the spring of 1990 companies in all the leading Western countries were reporting that Soviet enterprises were in arrears, in some cases for six months or more.[60] An increasing number of firms began to cut off further shipments until

59. Most of the reports regarding payments difficulties during the fall of 1989 did not emerge until early 1990, when Western firms chose to go public in an effort to get their money. See, for example, "Plan on Paying Overdue Bills Set by Soviets," *Wall Street Journal*, May 23, 1990, p. A20; and Laurie Hays and Peter Gumbel, "Soviet Concerns Falling Behind in Paying Bills," *Wall Street Journal*, March 6, 1990, p. A3.

60. See, for example, complaints by firms in Japan (Yumiko Ono, "Japanese Traders Informing Tokyo Soviet Bills Unpaid," *Wall Street Journal*, May 3, 1990, p. A15; and "Soviets Told That Payment Delays May Hit Funding," *Financial Times*, July 18, 1990, p. 3); in Britain and West Germany (Laurie Hays, "Payment Delays of Soviets Hurt Western Firms," *Wall Street Journal*, May 7, 1990, p. A11); and in Australia and New Zealand (Kevin Brown, "Moscow Asks Wool Exporters for Credit," *Financial Times*, May 8, 1990, p. 3).

outstanding accounts were settled.[61] By the end of May, Soviet leaders were acknowledging the crisis, admitting to arrears in the neighborhood of $2 billion, and they were asking for patience, as well as for short-term loans.[62]

Causes: The Official Explanation

The causes of this payments crisis are obscure, but certainly appear to be multiple. Stepun Sitarian, then deputy prime minister, and chairman of the State Foreign Economic Commission until May 1991, echoed the official view that three factors had precipitated the crisis: declining terms of trade; mistakes by newly independent, inexperienced traders; and the exaggerated noise made by a multitude of small Western firms that were suffering from delayed payments.[63] The last charge is the least serious, amounting to no more than a bureaucrat's complaint that the situation will be all right if the injured parties will stop fussing about it. The other two adduced causes deserve closer attention, although neither seems to have a great deal to do with the crisis.

There was a decline in Soviet terms of trade with the West during the second half of the 1980s, due primarily to the fall in oil prices. But, as table 3-3 shows, most of the decline came in 1986, thus predating the major foreign economic policy reforms. By the time the reforms took effect, Soviet terms of trade had settled down at about 80 percent of their 1980 level. And, as table 3-4 shows, although Soviet exports did drop in 1986 because of the unexpected decline in

61. Peter Montagnon, "Moscow Scrambles to Redeem Credit Rating," *Financial Times*, May 25, 1990, p. 4.

62. See the interview with Stepun Sitarian, the newly appointed head of the State Foreign Economic Commission, in "Platit' dolgi" (To pay debts), *Izvestiia*, May 22, 1990, p. 1. There were numerous reports of Soviet efforts to gain extensions in their short-term debt. See, for example, Brown, "Moscow Asks Wool Exporters for Credit," p. 3; and "Export-Credit Group Set to Discuss Delays in Soviet Payments," *Wall Street Journal*, May 22, 1990, p. A17.

63. Sitarian, "Platit' dolgi," p. 1. See also the brief statement of T. Alibegov, first deputy chairman of Vneshekonombank, "'Goriachaia liniia': 'EZh'—Vneshekonombank—chitatelie:" ('The hot line': *Ekonomika i zhizn'* —Vneshekonombank— readers), Ekonomika i zhizn', no. 28 (July 1990), p. 19.

Table 3-3. *Soviet Terms of Trade with Nonsocialist Countries, 1980, 1985–89*
1980 = 100

Item	1980	1985	1986	1987	1988	1989
Export prices	100	83	69	76	76	81
Import prices	100	80	85	88	99	101
Terms of trade	100	104	81	87	77	81

Source: "Soviet Foreign Trade Performance in 1989," *PlanEcon Report*, vol. 6 (May 25, 1990), p. 6.

Table 3-4. *Soviet Exports, Imports, and Balance of Trade with Capitalist Countries, 1980, 1985–90*
Billions of current dollars

Item	1980	1985	1986	1987	1988	1989	1990[a]
Exports	35.0	33.8	32.2	37.9	39.9	42.1	42.0
Developed West	24.4	22.3	18.6	22.5	24.2	26.1	27.6
Developing countries	10.6	11.5	13.6	15.5	15.8	16.1	14.4
Imports	32.0	32.3	29.5	29.5	35.7	43.6	42.9
Developed West	24.2	23.2	22.5	22.0	26.9	32.6	32.1
Developing countries	7.8	9.2	7.0	7.5	8.8	11.1	10.8
Balance of trade	3.0	1.5	2.7	8.4	4.2	− 1.5	− 0.7
Developed West	0.2	− 0.8	− 3.9	0.5	− 2.7	− 6.5	− 4.4
Developing countries	2.7	2.4	6.6	7.9	7.0	5.0	3.7

Sources: "Soviet Foreign Trade Performance in 1989," *PlanEcon Report*, vol. 6 (May 25, 1990), p. 29; "Soviet Foreign Trade Performance during the First Three Quarters of 1990," *PlanEcon Report*, vol. 6 (January 18, 1991), p. 10; and "Ekonomika SSSR v 1990 godu" (The Economy of the USSR in 1990), *Ekonomika i zhizn'*, no. 5 (January 1991), p. 13.
a. Data for first three quarters of 1990 only. Converted from valuta rubles at a rate of R1 = $1.59 (official rate).

export prices, they subsequently rebounded. Thus, to the extent that balance-of-payments pressures grew in the late 1980s, it was primarily because import demand accelerated in spite of the decline in terms of trade.

Sitarian's other serious charge—that newly independent traders contributed to this crisis through their inexperience— is difficult to assess, but seems unfounded. It was true that by late May 1990 more than 16,000 organizations were entitled to direct foreign trade rights, a veritable explosion relative to the 240 entities legally entitled to trade directly as of April 1, 1989.[64] And no doubt some of those organizations

64. Earlier figure is from earlier in this chapter; the May 1990 figure is from Sitarian, "Platit' dolgi," p. 1.

incurred debts they were unable to pay back. But payments problems had already begun to show up in the fall of 1989, well before many of the new entities were up and running, let alone able to incur debt and fall behind in paying it. Moreover, some Western bankers were reporting that their payments problems had originated not in the new small entities but in the large old Soviet traders such as Soiuzkhimeksport (chemicals), Exportkhleb (grain), and Promsyreimport (raw materials).[65] These were FTOs, still under the control of the Ministry of Foreign Economic Relations, and problems in their payments would seem to suggest it was Vneshekonombank, rather than the newly independent traders, that was the cause.

Causes: The Real Explanation

Although it is easy to dismiss the official story behind the balance of payments crisis, it is rather more difficult to understand what actually happened. Part of the answer certainly lies in the government's decision in 1988–89 to drastically increase imports of consumer goods in an effort to counteract the growing shortages in retail markets. Virtually all the $7.9 billion increase in imports from nonsocialist countries in 1989—which pushed the trade deficit to $6.5 billion—can be accounted for by the growth in imports of consumer goods.[66] Although these imports may have been financed in part by state-guaranteed credits from Western governments, it is likely that they were not fully

65. Quentin Peel, "Moscow Faces Import Payment Crisis," *Financial Times*, May 18, 1990, p. 2. See also the letter of a British banker, A. D. Cooper, to *Izvestiia* (July 29, 1990), which also suggests that the large FTOs were responsible for most of the payment delays. "Mnenie ekspertov" (Opinion of the experts).

66. A decision was taken at the end of 1988 to dramatically expand manufactured consumer goods imports in 1989, which probably resulted in a net increase in consumer goods imports in 1989 of approximately R2.5 billion, or $4 billion (estimate based on "Soviet Foreign Trade Performance in 1989," pp. 10, 21). See "Official Notes Purchase of Imported Consumer Goods," *Argumenty i fakty*, April 15-21, 1989, p. 8, in *Daily Report: SU*, April 18, 1989, p. 81; and T. Valovaia, "Strategiia: importa i eksporta" (The strategy: imports and exports), *Ekonomicheskaia gazeta*, no. 15 (April 1989), p. 20. Food imports went up by a similar amount, also directly targeted to the consumer market. Ibid., p. 21.

covered and therefore created cash flow problems for the Soviet banking system.[67] That, in turn, could have made it difficult for the large FTOs to get to their funds, or at least to get short-term credit from Vneshekonombank.

It is quite likely that Vneshekonombank contributed directly to the crisis, because it was either unable or unwilling to accommodate the newly independent trading entities. Vneshekonombank saw the number of accounts it had to service explode from several hundred to 16,000 in one year, and that would have been enough to throw even a well-oiled accounting system into chaos. Moreover, the Vneshekonombank officials were hardly subtle in their disdain for the new system of direct foreign trading rights, with its implications for their loss of control. It would not be surprising if they actually allowed the crisis to begin, but then lost control of it.[68]

Consequences for the Soviet Credit Rating

Although the reasons for the crisis are somewhat obscure, the results were clear and dramatic. By the summer of 1990 most Western banks had stopped lending to the USSR, except when they had a 100 percent credit guarantee. Worse yet, banks grew unwilling to even roll over the short-term credits that had normally been automatic.[69] In the space of little more than a year, the USSR had slipped from what was considered one of the best sovereign credit risks in the world to an unacceptably bad risk. It financed its expanding trade deficit in 1990 solely through gold sales and state-supported credits from the West. By the end of 1990, even those credits had dried up in response to the

67. Viktor Gerashchenko, chairman of Gosbank, did admit in an interview that one cause of the crisis was the Soviet government's "excessively ambitious export-import plan." Quentin Peel, "Moscow Faces Import Payment Crisis," *Financial Times*, May 18, 1990, p. 2.

68. Anecdotal evidence suggests that, at the very least, some of the payments delays came because Soviet enterprises with foreign exchange in their accounts could not get Vneshekonombank to release it. See, for example, *Wall Street Journal*, January 21, 1990, pp. A1ff.

69. Sitarian, "Platit' dolgi," p. 1.

conservative turn in political and economic reforms, and the payments crisis began to look chronic.

The Deeper Roots of the Disappointing Results

Even if the planning authorities had enthusiastically implemented the December 1988 decree, and even if the balance-of-payments problems had not emerged, it would have been remarkable if Soviet enterprises had responded with a burst of manufactured goods exports. These enterprises enjoyed such high domestic demand for their products that they had little incentive to go through the extra bother of developing foreign markets. A successful export strategy requires enormous effort and expense, and firms throughout the world resort to exports only when they find domestic markets shrinking. In the Soviet Union, particularly in the late 1980s as the government began to expand the money supply, the domestic market heated up for Soviet enterprises. In that environment there was no reason for them to spend much time searching for even more customers, particularly foreign customers.

For those enterprises that chose to export, despite the enormous institutionalized incentives not to do so, planners themselves presented yet another obstacle through state orders (*goszakazy*). Enterprises found it almost impossible to develop product lines for exports, because planners consciously set state orders as high as possible to obtain goods for the domestic market.

The common thread running through the various explanations for a disappointing response to the new reforms was the stalemate in general reforms. By 1989–90 that was the fundamental problem, not the bungling of a few bureaucrats. Moreover, 1989 was the year when the festering problems among Soviet nationalities began to take on true economic significance, contributing to a stalemate in the economic reform debate and to a growing sense of chaos in the system. By 1990 the conflict had become so complex and so serious that there were growing doubts anything could be done to avoid the disintegration of the country.

CHAPTER FOUR

Stagflation and Disunion

THE YEAR 1990 was arguably as important to the future of the USSR as 1985, the year Mikhail Gorbachev came to power. But unlike 1985, which had ushered in hope, 1990 brought despair. The seemingly complete failure of economic reforms coalesced with the already gloomy political atmosphere to create a sense of lost direction, chaos, and even disintegration. As a result, in the course of 1990 the world's perceptions of the direction of change in the USSR swung from virtually unbounded euphoria to extreme pessimism. Gorbachev's skillfully crafted campaign to enter the world economy began to unravel in the face of a reality that contradicted his words.

The crises of 1990 were all tied in with the economy. The government's reform measures of 1986–89, instead of presenting a coherent strategy, were uncoordinated and incomplete and could only lead to economic chaos. By 1990 the economy was in recession, with unmistakable signs that 1991 would be worse still.

These grave conditions merely strengthened separatist sentiments in the Baltic republics, and elsewhere. Republican leaders appealed for economic sovereignty, even for secession, to escape the apparent incompetence of central economic authorities. Whatever the costs of independence, they would be counterbalanced by the benefits of the republican governments' willingness to pursue a coherent strategy for creating free markets, unencumbered by the ideological baggage that burdened the center's approach to the economy.

In 1988 and 1989, when Estonia was most prominent in demanding economic independence, separatist tendencies were a peripheral issue in the debate over economic reform. Central authorities recognized the problem but considered it a second-level one that could be managed. By the summer of 1990, however, Boris Yeltsin was using his new post as chairman of the Russian parliament to push for Russian economic sovereignty and for a rapid move to a market economy. Matters came to a head in the fall of 1990, in the struggle over the so-called 500-Day Plan, which proposed that the USSR reform itself as a loose confederation committed to erecting the basic elements of a market economy in 500 days. Yeltsin's move transformed what had seemed to be a manageable problem into an unavoidable debate over the future of the system.

When the 500-Day Plan failed to be endorsed at the national level, a political and economic crisis of enormous dimensions ensued. The republics and the center engaged in a grim struggle for power that caught consumers, small businesses, and foreign investors in the middle. At the beginning of 1990 it was unmistakably clear that reforms in foreign economic relations would have little impact unless those on the domestic scene moved ahead. Yet by the end of 1990 domestic reforms were still in limbo.

The Path to Economic Crisis

The transformation that occurred in the Soviet economic system cannot be fully understood without some knowledge of two somewhat separate but interrelated series of events. The first story, the easiest to follow, concerns the increasingly radical reforms debated in the government, beginning with the June 1987 *Osnovnye polozheniia* (Basic theses), which constituted the first effort at a blueprint for comprehensive reform, and ending with the 500-Day Plan. This is the story of a bureaucracy reluctantly acquiescing to the notion that markets, not central planning, are the road to economic prosperity. In 1985 the question was how to modernize central planning. Five years later, that question almost forgotten, the issue was what sort of market economy the USSR should strive for, and what sort of transition strategy it should follow.

The second story, about what actually happened, is much more difficult to follow because the events took many unexpected turns. The government began to cede some control over the system through conscious decentralization, only to find that it was losing more control than it intended. Systemic change was occurring at the grass roots, but in ways unforeseen, and sometimes even unknown, by the center. Thus the decrees, although important, tell only part of the story. Even statistics are of limited assistance. The main details can be gleaned from the mass of anecdotes and news items about enterprises, republics, and individual deals that gave rise to an uncoordinated, sporadic, and partial marketization of the old system, with many unpleasant consequences.

The reform debates and the actual course of events revolved around the domestic economy, not foreign economic relations. Efforts on the foreign front, discussed in earlier chapters, seemed to be operating on a somewhat separate track, and certainly on a different timetable. But the domestic and global economies became entwined in the second half of the 1980s in ways that the center did not expect or fully understand. As the centrally directed reform process broke down, enterprises and local authorities suddenly found opportunities to participate in foreign economic relations through channels closed to them only a few years earlier.

A complete treatment of these reforms would go well beyond the limits of this book. The reform programs, the complex path of their sporadic implementation, and the great gulf between the actual system and that intended by the center all deserve their own books and will no doubt get them. For present purposes a general overview of the process will suffice to draw out its implications for foreign economic relations.

Reforms Reduced to the Bare Essentials

It is easiest to understand what went awry in the reform process of the second half of the 1980s by focusing on the few essential features of the system that underwent changes in those years. This treatment ignores the details not because they are irrelevant but because they are so massive that they can obscure the most important features of the reforms and of their consequences.

THE LOGIC OF THE OLD SYSTEM. The old system, as it existed in 1985, had four basic features: (1) a strong center, (2) a weak periphery, (3) fixed prices, and (4) strict controls over all contracts between the domestic and global economies.[1]

The center controlled all important aspects of economic activity mainly by micromanaging the system through Gosplan, the ministries, and the party apparatus. Strict controls on financial flows allowed the central authorities to accumulate capital and foreign exchange, which was then allocated according to centrally determined priorities. Although this control fell far short of the omnipotence the center yearned for, it was impressive in its ability to shape economic activity.

The logical counterpart of the strong center was a weak periphery. Enterprises operated under stifling controls in which the center—represented by the sectoral ministries—specified the mix of products produced; set strict limits on the uses of receipts, confiscating all that remained after those limited purposes were served; and maintained a tight hold on capital expenditures, and thus on the structure of additions to productive capacity. The state used an incredibly complex bonus scheme to encourage enterprises to fulfill ambitious central plans for outputs, inputs, and efficiencies. Republics, regional authorities (*oblasti, raiony*), and municipal authorities were extremely weak, essentially powerless to affect decisions of the center.

Prices and money were intentionally passive in this system, serving primarily an accounting function. Prices were set centrally, or at least according to centrally defined procedures, and were changed only periodically to reflect changing costs. Because prices were not intended as signals for what should be produced, there was no link between prices and supply and demand, nor were domestic and world market prices connected in any way. Money was used to keep track of enterprise activity, but it was only formally a means of payment. For an enterprise wishing to undertake a capital expansion, the first step was

1. For a discussion in much more detail, see Ed A. Hewett, *Reforming the Soviet Economy: Equality versus Efficiency* (Brookings, 1988), chaps. 3–4.

to seek central authorization, then to get the center to allocate the materials. When that was done, the actual transaction, accomplished in rubles, was a foregone conclusion. Thus, even internally, the ruble was not "convertible" into goods; in other words, for the enterprise sector, the ruble was not money.[2]

This system was consciously and effectively cut off from the world economy through the foreign trade monopoly, discussed in some detail in chapter 1. It had to be that way because of the structure of the system. Free trade with the outside world contradicted the internal arrangements that planners demanded. Planners had to decide on exports and imports if they were to control all economic activity. Free trade would have led to exports and imports contrary to planners' intentions. In fact, because domestic prices were unrelated to world market prices, free trade was impossible.

This extremely simplified description of the traditional system gives an inkling of its essential characteristic: the internally logical interconnections among its basic institutions. The strong center meant a weak periphery; central control over resource allocation meant that money was of secondary importance; central management of local production meant that prices were irrelevant; irrational prices and central controls meant that foreign trade had to be controlled by the center. To change any part of this system, while trying to retain the rest, was to violate the logic of the system and to risk disarray.

THE OSNOVNYE POLOZHENIIA. Nevertheless, that was precisely the course Mikhail Gorbachev embarked on in 1985 when he began his search for a variation of this system that would be capable of competing with developed countries on world markets. During 1985–86 reforms seemed to follow no particular strategy. They were haphazard and modest in scope, making no major change in the traditional system. But they set the tone for future years in their cavalier inconsistency. At the same time that enterprises were being given more leeway on paper to follow their economic instincts, Mikhail Gorbachev and his

---

2. The ruble was, in some sense, what an economist would call "money" in the consumer goods sector. It could be used to buy goods and could operate as a share of value, although in only a limited and imperfect fashion.

new prime minister, Nikolai Ryzhkov, were signing decrees ordering enterprises to increase quality, reduce costs, and so on.[3]

It was in 1988 that Mikhail Gorbachev launched the first serious effort to transform the traditional system in the hope of dramatically improving Soviet economic performance. The basic guiding document was the *Osnovnye polozheniia*, developed in the first half of 1987 by a network of committees composed of prominent economists and bureaucrats. Gorbachev presented the document to the June 1987 Party Plenum.[4] The laws implementing the *Osnovnye polozheniia*, which were also drafted in preparation for the June Plenum, began to come into effect in 1988.[5]

This, the first substantial effort to articulate a comprehensive reform strategy, was strongly influenced by the Andropov reforms of the early 1980s, but it also showed a clear disposition to accept more radical approaches to modernizing the Soviet economy. There was no mention of a market system. Rather, the idea was to modernize central planning by switching from administrative to so-called economic means of controls; that is, to use financial incentives rather than commands to guide enterprises toward the fulfillment of central wishes. This was not to be a revolutionary transformation of any of the four fundamental features of the traditional system, but a streamlining that would improve economic performance without threatening central control.

The centerpiece of the reform was a new arrangement whereby the

3. For a discussion of this period, see Hewett, *Reforming the Soviet Economy*, chap. 7.

4. "Osnovnye polozheniia korennoi perestroiki upravleniia ekonomikoi" (Basic theses for the radical restructuring of the management of the economy), *Pravda*, June 27, 1987, pp. 2–3. Gorbachev's discussion of the document is in "O zadachakh partii po korennoi perestroike upravleniia ekonomikoi: Doklad General'nogo sekretaria TsK KPSS M. S. Gorbacheva na Plenume TsK KPSS 25 Iiunia 1987 goda" (On the tasks of the party for the radical restructuring of the management of the economy: Report of the General Secretary of the CC of the CPSU M. S. Gorbachev to the plenum of the CC of the CPSU, June 25, 1987), *Pravda*, June 26, 1987, pp. 1–5. For an analysis of the *Osnovnye polozheniia*, see Hewett, *Reforming the Soviet Economy*, chap. 7.

5. *O korennoi perestroike upravleniia ekonomikoi: Sbornik dokumentov* (On the radical restructuring of the management of the economy: A collection of documents) (Moscow: Politizdat, 1987).

center ceded to the enterprises the power (although with considerable limitations) to decide on product mix; the structure of capital expenditures; the size, structure, and compensation of the labor force; and pricing. Instead of receiving comprehensive quotas covering all output, enterprises would receive *goszakazy* (state orders) for a portion of their output, but would have control over the remaining output decisions. Increasingly, inputs would be obtained through wholesale trade at prices negotiated according to elaborate rules amounting to regulated prices rather than through Gossnab's (State Committee for Material-Technical Supply) distribution system. Indeed, the regional organs of this system were to be transformed into profit-oriented wholesalers.

In addition, the entire relationship between the center and the enterprises regarding rewards for successful operation was restructured. The previous arbitrary and capricious bonus schemes for enterprises were regularized in agreements on norms specifying profit retention rights for enterprises. An enterprise that could figure out how to increase receipts by satisfying its consumers could keep a portion of those receipts without fear that its ministry would confiscate the proceeds, or so the law specified.

In exchange for these new rights enterprises were told that they would be held responsible for their own profitability and that the state would not bail them out. Enterprises producing 60 percent of industrial output came into this new system on January 1, 1988, and most of the remaining enterprises joined them in 1989.

Although there was no direct connection, some of the same enterprises that acquired greater autonomy in basic decisions on current and capital expenditures also gained the right to engage directly in foreign trade. In 1989, as the provisions of the new law spread to most enterprises, many also gained the right to direct foreign trading.

Anatomy of the Breakdown

As these reforms were implemented, it became clear that they were indeed departing from the traditional system. The central apparatus that had been used to manage enterprise activity in such detail at the local level was being reduced in power and size. By 1989 the ministerial bodies controlling the system employed just over 871,000 people, which was nearly 50 percent below the level of 1985, when Mikhail Gorbachev came to power, and nearly 30 percent below that of 1987, on the eve of the implementation of the reforms spawned by the *Osnovnye polozheniia*.[6] The number of ministries was reduced through mergers. The seventy-three key ministerial bodies that together oversaw the economy at the all-union and union-republic level in June 1987 had been merged into fifty-two entities by the end of 1989.[7]

Those ministerial staff reductions plus the new laws gave enterprises much more control over their activities than in the past. The switch from direct plan directives to state orders, for example, brought a fourteenfold reduction in the number of products distributed centrally by Gosplan and Gossnab in 1990 in comparison with 1987.[8] At the same time, various new laws, most notably the May 1988 law on cooperatives, encouraged the development of small enterprises and thereby broadened the entire economic system at the base. By the end of 1990 there were 245,000 cooperatives employing 6.1 million persons (more than 5 percent of the labor force) and contributing nearly 7 percent of GNP.[9] Thus by 1989–90 the system was more decentralized than it had been a few years before.

This reform package represented an immense improvement over previous efforts, both in its scope and in the degree of real change.

6. These staff reductions reflect not only direct cutbacks in the ministries but also a reorganization of a number of state management agencies into production enterprises. *Narodnoe khoziaistvo SSSR v 1989 g.: Statisticheskii ezhegodnik* (National economy of the USSR in 1989: Statistical yearbook) (Moscow: Finansy i statistika, 1990), pp. 49–50.

7. Figures for 1987 are from Hewett, *Reforming the Soviet Economy*, pp. 110–11. Central Intelligence Agency, USSR Council of Ministers: A Reference Aid (December 1989).

8. K. Malakhov, "Materialno-tekhnikcheskoye obespechenie narodnogo khozaistva" (Material-technical support of the economy), *Planovoe khozaistvo*, vol. 10 (October 1989), pp. 3–15; cited in James H. Noren, "The Soviet Economic Crisis: Another Perspective," in Ed A. Hewett and Victor H. Winston, eds., *Milestones in Glasnost and Perestroyka: The Economy* (Brookings, 1991), p. 381.

9. Goskomstat SSSR, Press-vypusk (Press release), no. 150, May 17, 1991; and Goskomstat SSSR, *Kratkii statisticheskii spravochnik, 1991* (Brief statistical abstract, 1991) pp. 7–9.

Nevertheless, it was fatally flawed in design and implementation. It focused primarily on the management and operation of state enterprises and paid insufficient attention to the rest of the system, most notably pricing, competitive conditions, and macroeconomic policy. The result was a set of unstable and inconsistent institutions in which economic units, suddenly given a degree of authority that they had never before enjoyed, were allowed to exercise that authority without adequate constraints on their behavior. There was also an excess of money, and the price system was totally divorced from economic reality.

DESIGN FLAWS. One serious problem in the design of the reform concerned prices. It was clearly understood, for example, that the prices prevailing in 1987–88 had to be changed, since they reflected neither cost nor demand and therefore sent the wrong signals to producers. But the *Osnovnye polozheniia* retained central control over prices and concentrated on the changes needed to put together the thirteenth Five-Year Plan (the central economic plan for 1991–95).[10] There was no sign of recognition that if enterprises were to have a say in outputs and inputs, they needed a flexible price system influenced by supply and demand—in other words, a set of market-determined prices.

Nor did anyone see that the new bonus schemes would hardly be sufficient to discipline large enterprises enjoying near monopolies, and therefore that a pro-competitive policy would be important to ensure that the new system would work. The *Osnovnye polozheniia* did extol the virtues of a rather tame form of competition (*sotiazatel'nost'*) between state enterprises and cooperatives. But the main thrust of the reform actually celebrated the large enterprise; and certainly there was no hint, for example, of the utility of competitive imports as a disciplining force in the new system.

POLICY MISTAKES. Even the flawed design might have imposed some discipline on the new enterprises, had not the actual implementation of the reforms, and other aspects of policy, conspired to make matters worse. Price revisions, which were supposed to be prepared early enough to be used for constructing the thirteenth Five-Year Plan

---

10. See, for example, Morris Bornstein, "Price Reform in the USSR: Comment on Shmelev," *Soviet Economy*, vol. 4 (October–December 1988), pp. 328–37.

(1991–95), were not introduced in time.[11] Thus the system could not manage even to produce new prices, which, while far from satisfactory guides to decentralized decisions by enterprises, would have probably been an improvement over existing prices. This, in turn, was one of the main drags on the foreign trade reforms, since the move away from the differentiated foreign exchange coefficients to real exchange rates and a meaningful tariff system was inconceivable without price revisions.

Cooperatives, which were basically small private enterprises, encountered irresistible temptations to make money on the irrational price system by buying cheap (at artificially low state prices) and selling dear (at much higher market prices). And even if they had not been thus tempted, the laws restricting access to materials, capital, or foreign exchange virtually forced them into such deals, and in particular into the black market. The entire cooperative movement grew unpopular as the government began looking for scapegoats. Thus over a few short years, cooperatives—which had been hailed in mid-1988 as the cutting edge of *perestroika*—were reviled as havens for criminals bent on stealing from honest wage earners.[12]

The new reforms came in the context of a virtually nonexistent framework for ensuring macroeconomic balance. In the old system no one had had to worry about the overall balance between aggregate demand and supply, because materials allocation provided a de facto microeconomic mechanism for managing the allocation of national product among the various end uses. In short, money did not matter.

In the new, decentralized system, in which enterprises made more of their own purchasing and sales decisions, money did begin to matter. Moreover, there was more money in the system. Perhaps most important, the budget deficit jumped from a fairly consistent 2–3 percent of GNP in the pre-Gorbachev era to nearly 8 percent of GNP in 1986 (because of the loss of government revenues in connection with Gorbachev's anti-alcohol campaign), and it topped 8 percent every year

11. Wholesale price changes finally came into effect on January 1, 1991.
12. Anthony Jones and William Moskoff, *Ko-ops: The Rebirth of Entrepreneurship in the Soviet Union* (Indiana University Press, 1991), esp. pp. 98–109.

through 1989. The government financed those deficits by printing money, thereby flooding the system with excess purchasing power.[13] Predictably, the large enterprises, many of which enjoyed a monopoly, acted to take advantage of the excess demand and the looser regulations. Although they could not freely set prices, they now enjoyed the right to choose their product mix. Since profit was calculated as a percentage of total cost, they responded by shifting their product mix toward more expensive product lines, or by introducing "new" products—the prices of which could by law be raised up to 30 percent over the previous models—in order to generate higher receipts. The result was both a higher overall price level and shortages of some goods (those discontinued, for example, because of low profitability).

Stagflation

The results of this bungled reform were already apparent in 1989 as growth rates fell well below those planned for 1986–90 (table 4-1). Only the year before, official statistics had shown national income growing faster than the planned rate for 1986–90. In 1990 the Soviet Union experienced the first decline in output in the postwar period. It is almost certain that these statistics include some hidden inflation, particularly from 1988 onward, when inflationary pressures grew. Therefore, the actual growth path for real output was surely lower and probably fell off much more sharply than these data indicate.

The mounting inflationary pressures are easy to detect in the official statistics. In 1988 the growth rate of wages shot up to 8.3 percent a year, while productivity grew at slightly less than 5 percent. In 1989

13. Strictly speaking, printed money covered only part of the deficit, since actual paper currency was directed only to the household sector in the form of wages and pensions. In the business sector, the money took the form of enterprise surplus balances. For a summary of the evolution of the budget deficits in the late 1980s and their causes, see Gur Ofer, "Budget Deficit, Market Disequilibrium, and Economic Reforms," in Hewett and Winston, *Milestones*, pp. 275–77.

Table 4-1. *Selected Economic Indicators for the USSR, Official Soviet Data, 1981–90*
Percent growth a year unless otherwise indicated

Item	1981–85	1986–90[a]	1986	1987	1988	1989	1990	1986–90
National income produced	3.2	4.1	2.3	1.6	4.4	2.5	−4.0	1.3
Labor productivity	2.7	4.2	2.1	1.6	4.8	2.3	−3.0	1.6
Freight transport	0.6	2.8	4.4	2.0	1.3	−1.9	−5.9	−0.1
New fixed capital brought on line	3.1	4.4	5.9	6.8	−1.4	2.5	−4.0	2.0
Per capita personal income	1.8	2.7	0.1	0.9	3.2	4.6	n.a.	n.a.
Budget deficit (billions of rubles)	17.6[b]	n.a.	51.9	66.2	79.0	92.0	58.1	69.4[b]
Average monthly wage	2.4	2.7	2.9	3.7	8.3	9.5	12.3	7.3
Savings deposits	7.1	n.a.	10.0	9.9	11.2	13.8	12.7	11.5
Hard currency debt								
CIA								
Gross	23.5[b]	n.a.	35.8	40.8	42.8	47	n.a.	n.a.
Net	11.8[b]	n.a.	20.9	26.4	27.3	32	n.a.	n.a.
IMF								
Gross	n.a.	n.a.	31.4	39.2	43.0	54.0	52.2	44.0[b]
Net	n.a.	n.a.	16.7	25.1	27.7	39.3	47.1	31.2[b]

Sources: Data through 1989 are from the statistical annual *Narodnoe khoziaistvo* for 1988 and 1989, published by Goskomstat, except the personal income growth for 1989, which is from the 1989 plan fulfillment report (*Pravda*, January 18, 1990, pp. 1–3). Data for 1990 are from the official Goskomstat plan fulfillment report published in *Ekonomika i zhizn'*, no. 5 (January 1991), pp. 9–13. The CIA estimate of debt is from CIA-DIA, ''The Soviet Economy Stumbles Badly in 1989,'' *JEC Testimony*, April 20, 1989, table C-8. For the IMF estimate of debt, see *The Economy of the USSR*, appendix table 2.
n.a. Not available.
a. The numbers in this column are from the five-year plan, not the actual numbers.
b. Five-year average.

wage growth accelerated once again, to 9.5 percent, while productivity growth fell to 2.3 percent, and the decline continued into 1990 as wage growth moved into the double digits.

The inflation of this period will require closer study as more data and anecdotal information become available. It was probably a fairly simple process: large state enterprises, which enjoyed virtual monopolies in their markets thanks to high protective barriers and a high concentration of domestic industry, exploited the excess demand they faced (the result of excess cash in the system) to effectively raise prices, therefore receipts, and therefore wages.[14] The government's role here was to run the printing presses to accommodate the inflation.

The decline in economic activity was accompanied by, and in part caused by, increasing shortages. Consumer goods shortages began to grow in 1985, and the situation grew much worse starting in 1988.[15] Because there was little consumers could do with their money, savings deposit growth rates climbed to 12–13 percent by 1989–90, even though interest rates in savings institutions averaged less than 3 percent (table 4-1). Industry, too, experienced shortages—in part because of the breakdown in shipments between the republics due to ethnic strife (for example, between Armenia and Azerbaijan).

Radicalization of the Reform Debate

As the crisis continued into 1989, the population grew ever more alarmed. In the remarkable summer of 1989 the newly created USSR Congress of People's Deputies engaged in a publicly televised catharsis over the state of the economy. When Prime Minister Ryzhkov brought

14. Technically, price controls were still in effect, but the new laws on contract pricing for new products provided a large loophole, since enterprises could declare a product "new" and force the higher prices on sellers who had no other alternative but to accept.
15. Noren, "Soviet Economic Crisis," pp. 373–76.

a slate of nominees for seventy posts in his newly revamped council of ministers, he was staggered to see the Congress reject eleven of his candidates, in part because of deputies' anger over the economy.[16]

The summer of 1989 also saw the first widespread strikes in living memory in the USSR, a clear warning to Soviet leaders that their slow and haphazard approach to the economy was not just harmful to performance—it was politically dangerous.[17] In the fall of 1989 socialism collapsed in Eastern Europe, in the process providing an unambiguous indictment of central planning as an economic system.

Against this dramatic backdrop, Mikhail Gorbachev moved to gain control of the situation by bringing Leonid Abalkin, the respected head of the Institute of Economics, into the government as head of a newly formed State Commission on Economic Reform.[18] Abalkin was charged with bringing order to the reform process and with devising more comprehensive measures capable of stabilizing the economy and truly reforming it. Abalkin began his work during the summer of 1989 and by the fall had drafted a set of recommendations, which, after considerable internal debate, was discussed at a huge conference in Moscow in November. The response was so negative that the package was not adopted, but it did influence later proposals and for that reason alone is an important intermediate step to consider in explaining the subsequent course of the reform debate, even to this day.

The Abalkin Reform Package

Academician Leonid Abalkin, and the team he assembled, brought to the reform process a coherence and sense of the importance of economic issues that had been lacking up to then. Traditionally reforms had been the purview of Gosplan, an economic planning agency with

16. Jerry F. Hough, "The Politics of Successful Economic Reform," *Soviet Economy*, vol. 5 (January–March 1989), p. 29.

17. Peter Rutland, "Labor Unrest and Movements in 1989 and 1990," *Soviet Economy*, vol. 6 (October–December 1990), pp. 345–84.

18. "O gosudarstvennoi komissii soveta ministrov SSSR" (On the State Commission of the Council of Ministers of the USSR), *Ekonomicheskaia gazeta*, no. 31 (July 1989), p. 16.

virtually no economists. Its leadership and staff were composed primarily of engineers, many of whom had served in enterprises during their early years. The Gosplan approach, not surprisingly, had concentrated on the enterprise and on the bureaucratic side of planning.

As an economist, Abalkin understood the issues differently, focusing instead on the price system, property rights, and the financial system— in other words, on those institutions that must coordinate enterprise decisions in a market. It was a major departure from the past, and an extremely hopeful sign, for Gorbachev to create a separate institution in charge of economic reform, to choose an economist for its chairman, and to give it prominence by appointing the chairman to the post of deputy prime minister. Possibly most remarkable of all is the fact that Gorbachev would even go to Abalkin, a man who had publicly quarreled with him and rebuked him at the 19th Party Conference in June 1988 over his lack of a reform strategy.[19]

HIGHLIGHTS. Abalkin's proposed reforms were indeed drastic.[20] Their cornerstone was what the report called "destatization" (*razgosudarstvlenie*) of property, a weak form of denationalization.[21] That was to be accompanied by an unequivocal transition over five years to a market economy in which competition would be strong (supported in part by tough antitrust regulations). Full-scale social guarantees—including income indexation and unemployment insurance—would soften, without negating, the effect on the population. Central planning, as it had

19. "Vystuplenie tovarishcha Abalkina, L. I." (Statement of comrade L. I. Abalkin), *Pravda*, June 30, 1988, pp. 3–4. Reprinted in Ed A. Hewett and others, "The 19th Conference of the CPSU and Its Aftermath," in Hewett and Winston, *Milestones*, pp. 229–33.

20. This section draws primarily on Ed A. Hewett, "Perestroika-'Plus': The Abalkin Reforms," *PlanEcon Report*, vol. 5 (December 1, 1989), pp. 48–49. The basic document outlining the Abalkin plan is "Radikal'naia ekonomicheskaia reforma: pervoocherednye i dolgovremennye mery" (Radical economic reform: first-priority and long-term measures), *Ekonomicheskaia gazeta*, no. 44 (October 1989), pp. 4–5.

21. *Razgosudarstvlenie* literally means to take property out of state hands, but not necessarily to give it to private individuals. Destatized property could be simply leased out; it could be given over to stockholders who themselves were state enterprises; or it could be sold to private individuals (which, in more recent Soviet usage, is generally referred to simply as *privatizatsiia*).

been practiced for six decades, would be replaced fairly quickly by an economic policy relying primarily on economic instruments.[22]

The price system was given due prominence, the goal being to free most prices by 1995, although the prices of critical materials would remain under central control. Even those, however, would be set to closely reflect relative world market prices. The financial system would be transformed with the introduction of a two-tiered banking system (a central bank and commercial banks), which would undertake the bulk of financial intermediation.

In addition, the Abalkin report recognized the need to move quickly to stabilize the economy. It recommended sharp reductions in the budget deficit (to be achieved in part by cutting centralized capital expenditures), income controls, and a massive effort to expand the output of consumer goods and thus attack shortages in that area from the supply side.

FOREIGN ECONOMIC RELATIONS. The Abalkin plan was the first Soviet reform package to deal explicitly, and in some ways sensibly, with foreign economic relations. Although this issue did not receive prominent attention in the plan, it was discussed, and—more important—was mentioned throughout, rather than treated as a seeming afterthought.

One of the explicit goals of the plan was to move to a convertible ruble and do away with the vast array of differentiated foreign exchange coefficients. It proposed foreign exchange auctions—which came into operation later in 1989—with the idea of increasing their frequency and size until eventually a foreign exchange market emerged. Wisely, the plan recognized that a strengthened ruble would be a result of, not a prelude to, a successful reform. Ruble convertibility, in other words, depended on a flexible price system in which prices approximated those on world markets.

---

22. The Abalkin plan still saw a role for administrative methods in controlling state enterprises in transportation, communications, energy, and the defense industries. Otherwise, it foresaw a transition over a five-year period to a system in which enterprises in private, or at least social, hands would operate on their own account in a market.

Direct foreign investment played an important role in Abalkin's strategy. He proposed that a law on direct foreign investment be adopted at the beginning of the transition so that by 1995 foreign products would be available to help expand the supply of goods on the Soviet market. The plan even mentioned integrating Soviet financial markets into world markets.

The spirit of the plan implied that imports would form an important element in the pro-competitive policy needed to build a well-functioning market. Integration into the world economy was considered a vital step toward successful economic reform.

THE LEGACY OF THE ABALKIN REFORM PACKAGE. As already mentioned, most political leaders and economic and party officials were not pleased with the Abalkin commission's reform proposals. Consequently, Prime Minister Ryzhkov, and to some extent Mikhail Gorbachev, distanced themselves from the report, and it did not generate a full set of new reform decrees. Nevertheless, its impact is evident in every subsequent government program proposed or announced in the government's effort to devise a credible reform strategy.

In December 1989 Nikolai Ryzhkov came to the Congress of People's Deputies with a plan for 1990 and the outline of a plan for 1991–95 that paid lip-service to many features of the Abalkin plan—most notably its goal of a regulated market economy.[23] In a much more comprehensive document in May 1990, the Ryzhkov government outlined steps for moving to a regulated market. Not only did this new document draw heavily on the Abalkin plan, but it had the help of the

---

23. "Effektivnost', konsolidatsiia, reforma—put' k zdorovoi ekonomike: Doklad N. I. Ryzhkova" (Effectiveness, consolidation, reform—the path to a healthy economy: Report of N. I. Ryzhkov), *Sotsialisticheskaia industriia* (Socialist industry), December 14, 1989, pp. 1–3. A careful reading of this document suggests that Ryzhkov was far less committed than the authors of the Abalkin plan to the market side of the regulated market economy. Aside from draconian measures to stabilize the economy, there were no specifics on how this regulated market economy would work, and the few hints provided generally suggest a lack of understanding of even the most fundamental requirements for a viable market system. To cite just one example, the report extolled the virtue of integrating the USSR into the world economy while calling for cutbacks in imports of any products that the USSR could produce on its own.

Reform Commission (of which Abalkin was chairman).[24] In particular, the influence of Abalkin's program can be seen in many individual measures introduced as laws or presidential decrees in 1990 and 1991: the foreign exchange auctions, the new direct foreign investment laws, the proposed strategy for indexation against inflation, the two-tiered banking system, and so on.

While these proposals were being debated, the economic decline was accelerating. And although the government seemed capable of debating endlessly, it was unable to act. When it did propose to act in conjunction with Ryzhkov's May 1990 report, it bungled in the worst way by leading off with a proposal to stabilize the system through drastic increases in retail prices, which were to be almost fully compensated by increases in income. Confidence in the government had fallen so low that Ryzhkov's proposal was rejected, and he was ordered to come back to the Supreme Soviet with a new plan by September 1, 1990.[25]

Debate over the Union

The economy was not the only focus of attention in these troubled times. Another debate was gathering steam over the nature of the union.

24. "Ob ekonomicheskom polozhenii strany i kontseptsii perekhoda k reguliruemoi rynochnoi ekonomike: Doklad Pravitel'stva SSSR na tret'iu sessiiu Verkhovnogo Soveta SSSR" (On the country's economic situation and the concept of a transition to a regulated market economy: Report of the government of the USSR to the third session of the Supreme Soviet of the USSR), May 1990. Although Leonid Abalkin was still involved in drafting this document, Yuri Masliukov—first deputy prime minister, and chairman of Gosplan—played the key role. Unlike the academician Abalkin, Masliukov was not an economist but an engineer by training, and his approach to reforms tended to be more conservative.

25. For Ryzhkov's original proposal, see "Ob ekonomicheskom polozhenii strany i kontseptsii perekhoda k reguliruemoi rynochnoi ekonomike" (On the country's economic situation and the concept of a transition to a regulated market economy), *Pravda*, May 25, 1990, pp. 1–4. For the Supreme Soviet's response, see "Postanovlenie Verkhovnogo Soveta SSSR: O kontseptsii perekhoda k reguliruemoi rynochnoi ekonomike v SSSR" (Resolution of the USSR Supreme Soviet: On the concept of a transition to a regulated market economy in the USSR), *Izvestiia*, June 16, 1990, p. 1.

It had begun fairly harmlessly as an effort by Gorbachev to shift responsibilities for some aspects of the economy to local governments. In calmer political times, and better economic situations, such an initiative might even have been welcomed by local authorities. By 1989, however, the combined effect of *glasnost'*, the economic crisis, and elections to the new USSR Congress of People's Deputies had transformed the issue of local autonomy into a larger question about the nature of the union itself. And by 1990 it had begun to dominate all political and economic discourse inside, and often outside, the USSR. A complex, even convoluted, struggle ensued over a bewildering barrage of union, republican, and local laws and decrees, many of which directly contradicted one another and brought on a storm of threats and counterthreats.

To recount this historic struggle would be far too ambitious a task for this short book. Nevertheless, the basic events need to be mentioned because of their profound implications for Soviet foreign economic relations. As the republics asserted their sovereign rights (and some their right to secede), they also demanded control over all economic activity within their borders and over all cross-border contacts. For some republics—most notably Estonia, but later also Ukraine and others—the logical consequence was that interrepublican trade would become international trade, on an equal footing with trade with any other country. Even the republics unwilling to go that far still asserted their sovereign right to hold on to and dispose of all foreign exchange earned by any entity within their borders, and to set regulations governing all aspects of the republic's foreign economic relations.

In this historic debate the fates of economic reform, foreign economic policy, and the future of the union came to be inextricably intertwined. There could be no clear policy on foreign economic relations or, for that matter, on economic reform, so long as the source of authority within the union remained in dispute.

Republican Khozraschet

Almost from the beginning Mikhail Gorbachev tried to find ways to give the republics and local authorities more responsibility for meeting the needs of consumers. One of his first acts in April 1985 was to order local governments to encourage greater production of consumer goods and services.[26] In July 1986 he sought once again to expand the authority of local governments in the production of local consumer goods and food, and at the same time to obligate them to encourage such production.[27] These rather tentative and ill-defined measures seemed to have sprung from at least two desires: to decentralize some of the responsibility for the population's welfare in order to decentralize some of the blame for the shortages, and to follow the more logical principle that local governments, since they were closest to their populations, could better perceive and meet local needs.

In the *Osnovnye polozheniia* the decentralization strategy became better defined and took on more purpose. The republics were to assume responsibility for constructing all social and cultural facilities in their areas (hospitals, schools, and the like), for satisfying demands for food, and for coordinating the activities of all enterprises in the production of consumer goods and services. To finance the expenditures associated with these new responsibilities, republican and local governments were given part of the assessments made on enterprises for the use of labor and natural resources, a portion of turnover tax revenue, and funds from several other sources.[28]

In the fall of 1988, in the course of Mikhail Gorbachev's maneuverings to receive approval for the new constitution establishing the USSR Congress of People's Deputies, five of the republics threatened to boycott the deliberations, protesting that the new effort at decen-

26. "O merakh po dal'neishemu razvitiiu mestnoi promyshlennosti v 1986–1990 godakh i v period do 2000 goda" (On measures for the further development of local industry in 1986–1990, and in the period to the year 2000), *Sotsialisticheskaia industriia*, April 30, 1985, p. 1. (Decree approved April 18, 1985.)

27. "O merakh po dal'neishemu povysheniiu roli i usileniiu otvetstvennosti Sovetov narodnykh deputatov za uskorenie sotsial'no-ekonomicheskogo razvitiia v svete reshenii XXVII s''ezda KPSS" (On measures for further increasing the role and strengthening the responsibility of Soviets of people's deputies for the acceleration of social-economic development in light of the decisions of the Twenty-seventh Congress of the CPSU), *Izvestiia*, July 30, 1986.

28. "Osnovnye polozheniia korennoi perestroiki upravleniia ekonomikoi," and *O korennoi perestroike upravleniia ekonomikoi*, pp. 208–35.

tralization was too limited. Estonia, in particular, demanded control over all its own resources. Gorbachev sought to defuse the situation by agreeing to establish a constitutional committee to revise the center-republic relationship, a sufficient compromise to temporarily stave off the revolt.

THE CENTER'S EFFORTS TO DEFINE THE LIMITS. The new effort culminated in a draft law, published in mid-March 1989, on republican *khozraschet*, or, roughly, republican self-finance. This document set the tone for the government's general approach to union-republic relations.[29] It proposed dividing responsibilities along the lines suggested in the *Osnovnye polozheniia* but provided considerably more detail concerning who would have what authority over specific sectors and enterprises, and where the republics would obtain stable sources of income. The basic deal remained the same: republics were to take full responsibility for food, social services, light industry, and some parts

29. "Obshchiie printsipy perestroiki rukovodstva ekonomikoi i sotsial'noi sferoi v soiuznykh respublikakh na osnove rasshireniia ikh suverennykh prav, samoupravleniia i samofinansirovaniia" (General principles of restructuring the management of the economy and social sphere in the union republics on the basis of expanding their sovereign rights, self-management, and self-financing), *Pravda*, March 14, 1989, pp. 2–3.

The term *khozraschet* has no simple counterpart in English. When applied to an enterprise, it generally means that the enterprise finances its own operations out of revenues, including its capital investments. But it is consistent with *khozraschet* for an enterprise to operate at a planned loss. For a republic, the term was meant to convey the idea that the government would have responsibilities in well-defined areas and that it would meet them within the means available to it.

Although this particular draft of the law failed when it was finally brought to a vote in the fall of 1989, the government succeeded later in passing a not significantly different version in April 1990. "Zakon Soiuza Sovetskikh Sotsialisticheskikh Respublik: Ob osnovakh ekonomicheskikh otnoshenii Soiuza SSR, soiuznykh i avtonomnykh respublik" (Law of the Union of Soviet Socialist Republics: On the foundation of economic relations of the Union of Soviet Socialist Republics, Union, and Autonomous Republics), *Ekonomika i zhizn'* (Economy and Life), no. 17 (April 1990), p. 17. Later that month a closely related law was passed with the addition of a formal right for secession, but no procedures. "Zakon Soiuza Sovetskikh Sotsialisticheskikh Respublik: O razgranichenii polnomochii mezhdu Soiuzom SSR i sub"ektami federatsii" (Law of the Union of Soviet Socialist Republics: On the delineation of powers between the Union of Soviet Socialist Republics and the subjects of the federation), *Izvestiia*, May 3, 1990, pp. 1–2.

of construction, while the center retained control over heavy industry, fuels, raw materials, and the infrastructure. Moreover, the center would remain in full control of all aspects of economic policy: the general policy on pricing, wages, social insurance, foreign economic activity, and the budget. The republics were guaranteed certain tax receipts to cover the expenses of various economic activities on their territory. Any subsidies for products that were republican responsibilities (for example, food) would have to come out of those revenues.

In some ways this was a radical change. The draft contained estimates, for example, showing that adoption of the law would give many republics control over three-fourths or more of the industrial capacity in their areas, depending on the weight of agriculture and light industry in the economy of the republic.[30]

FOREIGN ECONOMIC RELATIONS.   The proposal for republican *khozraschet* kept foreign economic relations almost totally in the purview of the center, governed by the all-union regulations discussed in chapter 3. There was no room here for the notion that foreign exchange earned in a republic should stay there (although the republic could claim 5 percent of currency retained by enterprises within its borders). These were all-union matters, and the draft made no suggestion that that situation should change.

The Estonian Challenge to Republican Khozraschet

For the Baltic republics, especially for Estonia, this proposal was too little too late. First of all, although the center "granted" certain limited rights to the republics, it retained control over all major aspects of its relationship with them. Estonian leaders thought it should be the

---

30. The calculations showed, for example, that the Baltic republics would shift from controlling 7–9 percent of their industrial capacity to something approaching 57–72 percent. The RSFSR, where heavy industry and fuels were important, would only see an increase from a pre-law share of 4 percent to about 27 percent. "Obshchie printsipy perestroiki rukovodstva ekonomikoi i sotsial'noi sferoi v soiuznykh respublikakh na osnove rasshireniia ikh suverennykh prav, samoupravleniia i samofinansirovaniia," p. 2.

other way around. Moreover, they asked why the center should be keeping the best of the economy for itself—the high-priority, high-tech industries—while "giving" the republics the sectors of lowest priority and in the greatest difficulty. The Estonians wanted a different deal, as did the other Baltic republics. The debate intensified in 1989, when other republics began objecting to the center's approach, and by the fall—just as the economic reform debate was heating up—momentum had begun gathering for a genuine renegotiation of the basic structure of the union.

ESTONIA FOR ESTONIANS. Estonia's basic view, outlined in several official documents circulated during May and June 1989, was that it owned everything within Estonian borders, in the airspace above, and on the adjacent continental shelf. Logically, therefore, Estonia should be able to control all economic activity within its borders and benefit from the results of that activity.[31] This claim extended to all state enterprises, which were controlled at the time by Moscow-based ministries and were run by and large by Russian-born, Moscow-appointed managers.

The regulations by which the Estonians proposed to assume these rights were labeled "cost accounting" (*khozraschet*), but they were in fact a thinly disguised declaration of economic independence. The draft laws asserted the precedence of Estonian over Soviet law and the right of Estonia to determine the nature of its economic system; to issue its own currency; to control prices, wages, and investment; and to control migration. The draft allowed for the existence of "all-union"

---

31. The basic documents outlining the Estonian concept are "Concept of Cost Accounting in Estonia SSR," *Sovetskaia Estoniia*, May 23, 1989, pp. 2–3, in Foreign Broadcast Information Service, *Daily Report: Soviet Union*, June 19, 1989, pp. 100–13 (hereafter *Daily Report: SU*); "Law of the Estonian Soviet Socialist Republic: 'The Foundations of Economic Accountability of the Estonian SSR,'" *Sovetskaia Estoniia*, May 23, 1989, pp. 1, 4, in *Daily Report: SU*, June 12, 1989, pp. 62–67 (a law dated May 18, 1989; designed to implement the basic concept); and "On the Transfer of the Estonian Soviet Socialist Republic to Republic Cost Accounting (Economic Independence)," *Sovetskaia Estoniia*, May 23, 1989, p. 4, in *Daily Report: SU*, June 19, 1989, pp. 83–84.

property in Estonia, or the property of other republics and foreign states, which would be regulated by contracts and agreements.

The basic logic behind these demands was quite simple. If, Estonian leaders argued, they were to be held responsible for the welfare of Estonian residents, then they should have control over economic activity in Estonia.[32] And they were willing to take care of their own finances, their own budget, hard currency balance of payments, subsidies, and so on. Left to their own devices, they said, they could undoubtedly handle their own affairs better than Moscow had done, and therefore Estonian residents (citizens) would be better off for it.

FOREIGN ECONOMIC RELATIONS. The Estonian proposals would have essentially eliminated Soviet foreign economic policy, replacing it with republican foreign economic policy. Estonia's relations with the remaining fourteen republics were to be constructed in a fashion closely paralleling the old system under the Council for Mutual Economic Assistance (CMEA), in which the individual states governed their bilateral relations primarily through bilateral agreements within a formalistic and more or less irrelevant framework.[33] Estonia might choose to join other republics in unionwide projects (relating to the energy system, for example), but participation would be voluntary and the projects managed cooperatively. Put simply, the economic relationship between Estonia and the other Soviet republics would be that of sovereign nations.

More generally, Estonia would have its own currency, its own tariffs, and its own prices, which—by implication—would approach world market prices. Estonia would become a very small, very open economy. At the beginning its most important trade partner would undoubtedly be the rest of the Soviet Union, particularly Russia. But

32. In addition to the documents listed in note 31, see the interesting interview with Rein Otsason, one of the economists most deeply involved in developing Estonia's plans for economic independence: "Zhit' po sredstvam, otvechat' za sebia" (To live according to one's means, answer for oneself), *Sotsialisticheskaia industriia*, June 24, 1989, pp. 1–2.

33. See, for example, Otsason, "Zhit' po sredstvam," for an explicit reference to the CMEA as a model for Estonia's relations with the remainder of the USSR.

it was clear that over time Estonia hoped to use its independence to find a niche in the European market.

The Center's Response

As the Estonian challenge resonated throughout the other republics, central authorities began fervently defending the union structure. The proposed breakup, they warned, would be a disaster because of the close integration of the economy, and it would directly contradict current global trends toward increased integration (notably, in the European Community).[34] Admittedly, close integration did exist (although it was more within ministries than at the overall level of the economy), and current trends in the global economy do favor integration. The key point of Estonia's argument, however, was not that its economy could go it alone and therefore should not be integrated with a larger economy. Rather, the Estonians were convinced that they were linked to a collapsing economy and therefore that they would be better off—whatever the short-term costs—to strike out on their own in a quick maneuver to begin the process of integrating with the world economy.

Central authorities countered that the short-term costs, and maybe the long-term costs, would be too high. In late 1989 and 1990 analyses began to appear suggesting that virtually all the non-Russian republics were running trade deficits with the union as a whole (essentially with Russia) when the goods moving among republics were treated as exports and imports valued in current, domestic prices. Moreover, an estimate of the value of those trade flows in world market prices showed that every republic except Russia was running a significant deficit, which—of course—it would have to immediately cover if it achieved economic independence.[35] According to these data, Estonia's imports

34. For an early version of this argument, see E. Primakov, "Regional'nyi khozras-chet: Opyt i problemy" (Regional self-finance: experience and problems), *Pravda*, December 7, 1988, p. 4.

35. See, for example, Iurii Rytov and V. Grishchenko, "Soiuznye respubliki: Kto komu dolzhen?" (Union republics: Who owes whom?), *Pravitel'stvennyi vestnik* (Government herald), no. 5 (January 1990), pp. 6–7; and "Ob"em vvoza i vyvoza pro-

(from other republics and the world) in 1988 equaled 3.2 billion valuta rubles (approximately $5.5 billion) in world market prices, but exports amounted to only 1.9 billion valuta rubles (approximately $3.2 billion). If Estonia became independent, it would immediately be faced with a potential deficit of $2.3 billion.

Although these arguments did little to discourage the republics from seeking greater autonomy, they did have an unintended consequence of immense importance in highlighting Russia's pivotal role as the main source of subsidies and foreign exchange for the union. The challenge from Estonia, and for that matter from all the Baltic states, was a nuisance, but a manageable one. But a challenge from Russia posed a direct and potentially fatal threat to the center's efforts to limit decentralization.

The Russian Challenge

Because the Soviet Union was dominated by Russians, the Russian Republic had been simply left out of much of the edifice Soviet leaders had constructed to exercise their total control over other republics. There was no Russian Communist party, no Russian Komsomol, and no Russian Academy of Sciences.

In a sense, Russia's economic and political institutions were so central to the USSR that the absence of such institutions was understandable. Russia accounted for three-fifths of the USSR's national product, one-half of its population, 90 percent of its oil production, and three-fourths of natural gas production.[36] In many ways the Russian economy virtually *was* the Soviet economy, and—in the old system—

---

duktsii po soiuznym respublikam za 1988 g. vo vnutrennikh i mirovykh tsenakh'' (The volume of imports and exports by union republics for 1988, in domestic and world prices), *Vestnik statistiki* (Statistical bulletin), no. 4 (April 1990), pp. 49–60.

36. For a useful quick reference to the role of the Russian economy in the Soviet economy, see "Udel'nyi ves RSFSR v SSSR po osnovnym pokazateliam ekonomicheskogo i sotsial'nogo razvitiia" (The relative share of the RSFSR in the USSR by basic indicators of economic and social development), *Argumenty i fakty* (Arguments and facts), no. 20 (May 19–25, 1990), p. 3.

it was not terribly important that the Russian-Soviet economy was run by Soviet institutions.

Amid the clamor over republican institutions and over the division of rights and responsibilities between the center and the periphery, Russia itself began demanding sovereignty.[37] In 1990 its citizens formed the Russian Communist party under the leadership of Ivan Polozkov, who introduced a decidedly conservative, Russian nationalist tone to the debate over the future of the union.[38]

RUSSIAN SOVEREIGNTY UNDER BORIS YELTSIN. By far the most important events in the increasingly assertive Russian stance were the elections to the new Russian Supreme Soviet and the subsequent election of Boris Yeltsin on May 29, 1990, to the chairmanship of that body. Under Yeltsin's leadership the Russian Supreme Soviet moved quickly to stake out a position on sovereignty that supported many, although not all, parts of the Estonian approach.

As soon as the Russian Supreme Soviet was convened, its members issued decrees that echoed the radicalism of the Baltic states. Most notable was the declaration of Russian sovereignty of June 14, 1990, which asserted the supremacy of Russian over Soviet law and claimed for Russia the control of all property within its vast borders.[39] Ten days later the Russian Supreme Soviet issued a proposal outlining principles for a new union treaty that would unambiguously confirm

37. See, for example, Roman Solchanyk, "'A Strong Center and Strong Republics': The CPSU's Draft 'Platform' on Nationalities Policy," *Report on the USSR*, vol. 1 (September 1989), pp. 1–4.

38. Regarding the founding of the Russian Communist party, see "Postanovlenie uchreditel'nogo s''ezda kommunisticheskoi partii rossiiskoi sovetskoi federativnoi sotsialisticheskoi respubliki ob obrazovanii kommunisticheskoi partii RSFSR" (Resolution of the constituent congress of the communist party of the Russian Soviet Federated Socialist Republic on the foundation of the communist party of the RSFSR), *Izvestiia*, June 22, 1990, p. 1. For details of Polozkov's election, see "Uchreditel'nyi s''ezd kommunisticheskoi partii RSFSR: informatsionnoe soobshchenie" (Constituent congress of the Communist party of the RSFSR: information report), *Pravda*, June 24, 1990, p. 1.

39. "Deklaratsiia o gosudarstvennom suverenitete Rossiiskoi Sovetskoi Federativnoi Sotsialisticheskoi Respubliki" (Declaration of the state sovereignty of the Russian Soviet Federated Socialist Republic), *Sovetskaia Rossiia* (Soviet Russia), June 14, 1990, p. 1.

116   OPEN FOR BUSINESS

Russia's sovereignty, along with the sovereignty of all the other republics.[40] The center would still oversee defense and defense industries, the transport and communications systems, and energy distribution,
but all else would come under the control of Russia. The decree also
declared that Gosbank (the State Bank) would be subordinate to the
Russian Supreme Soviet, as would the ministries controlling the oil
and gas industry (recently combined) and capital construction in those
industries.

From the beginning Boris Yeltsin made it clear that he intended to
use Russian sovereignty to move quickly to a market economy, whether
or not Mikhail Gorbachev was ready to go along. His government,
announced in July, included several of the most articulate advocates
of market economies: Grigorii Yavlinsky as deputy prime minister and
chairman of the Russian Commission on Economic Reform (counterpart to the Abalkin Commission, from whence Yavlinsky came); Boris
Fedorov as minister of finance; and Mikhail Bocharov as chairman of
the Supreme Economic Council.

Yeltsin and his team set to work on a plan for moving quickly to
a market economy, at the same time maintaining public pressure on
Gorbachev for a commitment to such a move at the national level. In
a blizzard of decrees and counterdecrees that threatened to paralyze
the country, Russia and the union engaged in an acrimonious and
escalating battle for control of the economy.

By July the pressure was so strong that Gorbachev agreed to try to
work out a plan that he and Yeltsin could both support, the result being
the 500-Day Plan, of which more below.

RUSSIAN FOREIGN ECONOMIC RELATIONS. The Russian Supreme Soviet asserted its right to control Russian foreign economic relations as
a natural extension of its sovereignty. In July 1990, as part of the first

40. "Postanovlenie S''ezda narodnykh deputatov Rossiiskoi Sovetskoi Federativnoi Sotsialisticheskoi Respubliki: O razgranichenii funktsii upravleniia organizatsiiami
na territorii RSFSR (Osnova novogo Soiuznogo dogovora)" (Decree of the Congress
of People's Deputies of the Russian Soviet Federated Socialist Republic: On the
delimitations of the functions of management of organizations on the territory of the
RSFSR (A foundation for a new Union Treaty), *Sovetskaia Rossiia*, June 24, 1990,
p. 1.

salvo of Russian decrees and laws, the Russian Supreme Soviet declared the right of all Russian entities to engage in foreign economic relations (no matter who "owned" them) and committed itself to attracting foreign investment.[41] Unlike Estonia, Russia did not immediately commit itself to creating its own currency, opting rather for a convertible ruble. But the Supreme Soviet did order several of its committees to draft decrees designed for the "protection of the foreign exchange interests of the RSFSR."[42] At the same time, the Russian Supreme Soviet asserted its new rights by authorizing the creation of special economic zones in the RSFSR, in the process ignoring the various decrees and plans of the union government concerning these zones.[43]

This and other decrees sparked a conflict with central authorities over the limits to sovereignty, which came to be known as "the battle of the laws." Aside from a full-scale battle over who would control the banks, the fiercest disagreement concerned who should control foreign economic relations.[44]

Although many important issues were raised here, by far the most critical was who would control the oil, gas, gold, diamonds, and other key commodities located in Russia, which had formed the backbone of hard currency receipts for the USSR. Things came to a head in late

41. "Ob osnovnykh printsipakh osushchestvleniia vneshneekonomicheskoi deiatel'nosti na territorii RSFSR" (On the basic principles for conducting foreign economic activity on the territory of the RSFSR), *Sovetskaia Rossiia*, July 20, 1990, p. 1.

42. "Ob osnovnykh printsipakh osushchestvleniia vneshneekonomicheskoi deiatel'nosti."

43. "O sozdanii zon svobodnogo predprinimatel'stva" (On the creation of free enterprise zones), *Sovetskaia Rossiia*, July 19, 1990, p. 1.

44. Russia's efforts to take over Gosbank and to close the offices of the state savings banks led to a direct order from Viktor Gerashchenko on July 23 ordering all banks in the RSFSR to ignore the orders of the republican Gosbank. The battle continued, although the new bank laws approved at the union and Russian levels in late 1990 were evidently informally coordinated in such a way that they reduced considerably the potential for conflict between Russia and the center. Konstantin Rosev and Nikita Vadimov, "Soiuznyi Zakon o bankakh: eshche khuzhe, chem rossiiskii— dlia partkomov i Sovetov" (The union law on banks: Even worse than Russia's—for the party committees and soviets), *Kommersant* (Merchant), no. 48 (December 10–17, 1990), p. 4.

July when the Soviet government announced it had signed an agreement
with Central Centenary (a newly created Swiss subsidiary of DeBeers)
in London to market Soviet rough-cut diamonds exclusively for the
next five years. The deal had an estimated value of $5 billion. In
immediate exchange for the shipment of the current stock of Soviet
rough-cut diamonds, DeBeers extended a $1 billion loan, apparently
to support the modernization of the diamond industry.[45]

Within three weeks the Russian Supreme Soviet had moved to in-
validate that contract in a far-reaching decree that declared null and
void any agreements made without its consent since June 14 (the date
of the sovereignty declaration) concerning Russian diamonds and a
long list of other products, including all significant exports of precious
metals, energy, and raw materials.[46] The same decree warned that
Russia would not feel itself bound by any credit or other agreements
regarding these commodities that were signed without the consent of
the Russian Supreme Soviet. A few days later Viktor Yaroshenko,
chairman of Russia's Foreign Economic Commission (equivalent to
the GVK, chaired by Stepun Sitarian) announced Russia's desire to
join OPEC, in light of the fact that Russia was one of the world's
major oil producers.[47]

This conflict between Russian and Soviet authorities was, in objective terms, extremely one-sided. Both could issue decrees, but the
union authorities had the staff in place and the institutions (for example,
the KGB, the army, and customs service) under sufficient control to
frustrate the Russian government's efforts to wrest control of the economy. Nevertheless, by August this conflict was threatening to tear the

45. Kenneth Gooding, "Moscow in $5 Bn Diamond Agreement with DeBeers,"
Financial Times, July 26, 1990, p. 1. The deal was negotiated on the Soviet side by
Glavalmazzoloto, a foreign trade organization with a monopoly in the marketing of
diamonds and gold.

46. "O zashchite ekonomicheskoi osnovy suvereniteta RSFSR" (On the defense
of the economic basis of the sovereignty of the RSFSR), *Sovetskaia Rossiia*, August
14, 1990, p. 2. See also "Zaiavlenie" (Declaration), *Sovetskaia Rossiia*, August 17,
1990, p. 3, in which key members of the Russian Supreme Soviet discuss in some
detail the legal case for Russia's assertion of sovereign rights over the union.

47. "Russians Want to Join OPEC," *Washington Post*, August 21, 1990, p. D1.

union apart. Russian authorities might not be able to actually do much, but they could make it difficult for union authorities to do anything either. It was no longer clear who owned what, or who controlled what economic activity. Western firms engaged in foreign commerce with the USSR, particularly in foreign investment, feared they might get caught between the warring factions and suffer significant losses. As the crisis reached an even higher pitch, confidence in the Soviet government—indeed in any government on Soviet soil—evaporated.

The 500-Day Plan

By the summer of 1990 virtually everyone inside and outside the USSR could see that the country was in the grips of a profound crisis that was paralyzing its economy, its political institutions, and its leadership. The economic recession was deepening and inflation accelerating. Relations between the republics and the central and republican leaderships were extraordinarily tense, with Lithuania still under economic blocade and Russia rolling up its sleeves for a showdown. The government of Nikolai Ryzhkov, rebuffed when it brought a plan for economic stabilization and reform to the Supreme Soviet in May, was making little headway on the new version it was expected to present in September.

Boris Yeltsin had become the focal point of the crisis and of the hopes of those who felt he might know a way out. He used his new post as chairman of the Russian Supreme Soviet to preach the virtues of a market economy, arguing that he (unlike Nikolai Ryzhkov) knew how to introduce a market without reducing living standards and how to do it quickly—in 500 days. His message, however improbable, captured the attention not only of Soviet society, which had lost faith in the official ideology, but also of officials who seemed determined somehow to salvage it. Moreover, because Yeltsin had some of the USSR's best economists working on his economic program, even fairly cynical intellectuals—including some who had advised Mikhail Gorbachev—began to believe that Yeltsin's solution was possible and that it was the way out.[48] Mikhail Gorbachev, exhibiting the flair he had shown so often since 1985, agreed in late July to join his advisers with Yeltsin's in an attempt to devise a single plan acceptable to both leaders. The joint commission, under the leadership of Presidential Council member Stanislav Shatalin, met throughout August, presenting its report—*Perekhod k rynku* (Transition to the market)—to President Gorbachev and Chairman Yeltsin at the beginning of September.[49]

Key Elements of the 500-Day Plan

The 500-Day Plan was in most ways a logical outgrowth of the aspirations of the republics for genuine sovereignty in a viable economic system. It proposed that the USSR reconstitute itself as a confederation (through a new union treaty) in which all power would flow from the republics, which would govern through an Interrepublican Economic Council. That council, on which each republic would be represented equally, would govern the country through a much reduced set of all-union bodies responsible for those few functions the republics agreed could best be managed at the center: defense, foreign affairs, the environment, and the regulation of prices for key products of national significance. For the remainder, essentially for the core of the economy, including taxing and spending power, the republics would set policy.

The newly formed and totally voluntary confederation would, ac-

48. The two most prominent members of Yeltsin's team were Boris Fedorov, Russia's minister of finance; and Grigorii Yavlinsky, chairman of the Economic State Reform Commission for the Russian Republic. Earlier in 1990, while working on the USSR Reform Commission for Leonid Abalkin, Yavlinsky had worked with several colleagues to develop a 400-day plan that contained many elements later adopted in the 500-Day Plan. G. A. Yavlinskii, A. Iu. Mikhailov, and M. M. Zadornov, *400 dnei doveriia* (400 days of confidence) (Moscow: Nedra, 1990).

49. Rabochaia gruppa, obrazovannaia sovmestnym resheniem M. S. Gorbacheva i B. N. Yel'tsina (Working group, established by the joint decision of M. S. Gorbachev and B. N. Yeltsin), *Perekhod k rynku* (Transition to the market) (Moscow: Arkhangel'skoe, August 1990), pts. 1 and 2. For a more detailed discussion of this plan than is necessary here, see Hewett, "The New Soviet Plan," *Foreign Affairs*, vol. 69 (Winter 1990–91), pp. 146–67.

cording to the plan, then move within 500 days to introduce a market economy in what would in effect be an economic union, with free internal trade and a common external tariff.[50] The main policy measures, outlined in four phases—an initial 100-day phase, two 150-day phases, and a final 100-day phase—provided for a total dismantling of the administrative system; *razgosudarstvlenie*, but also privatization; the removal of price controls and a transition to free prices; a drastic budget reduction to stabilize the economy; the establishment of an extensive banking system; and a strong system of unemployment insurance and income redistribution. Many of the ideas in the 500-Day Plan could be traced back to those originally proposed in the Abalkin program and then carried forward to the more recent governmental programs supported by the Ryzhkov government. Two important differences were the speed with which the 500-Day Plan would move and the commitment to privatization.

Most important, however, was the commitment of the 500-Day Plan to a confederation. Under the plan the Ryzhkov government would have disappeared, and most of its ministries would have been eliminated as the constituent enterprises were first "destatized" and then privatized. President Gorbachev and the USSR Supreme Soviet would have seen a dramatic reduction in their powers, because the new supreme authority was to be the Interrepublican Economic Council, headed by a president elected from among the members of the council.

Foreign Economic Relations under the 500-Day Plan

A stated goal of the 500-Day Plan was to open the Soviet economy to the world economy in order to accelerate economic reform and also to soften the impact of the transition. There was also a commitment to use imports as a competitive force in the system.[51] This was the first reform proposal ever put forth in the USSR to aim so explicitly

---

50. From the beginning the authors of the plan understood it would take much longer than 500 days to do what they intended to do. But 500 days was a good start, and certainly a catchy number with political appeal.

51. This account is based on *Perekhod k rynku*, pt. 1, sec. 7, pp. 112–23.

and fully at opening the Soviet economy to the world economy, and to do so for the right reasons.

This was also the first first comprehensive statement of how foreign economic relations might be managed in a system in which the republics enjoyed true sovereignty, yet the country retained a single currency and a single external tariff. It was in effect the Russian, not the Estonian, version of how foreign economic relations should work. The plan retained the State Foreign Economic Commission, its job being to implement national goals in foreign economic policy. A tariff authority would enforce a single tariff system for the entire country. The exchange rate would be uniform, devalued from its current rate, as determined in exchanges that would evolve over time into a true market. A newly formed Reserve Bank, patterned on the U.S. Federal Reserve, would manage the foreign exchange market.

Most foreign-trading activity would be conducted by enterprises, which would be either private or at least publicly held corporations (except in the case of fuels, raw materials, and some other key products, which would remain in the hands of confederation or republican authorities). Enterprises would be required to sell a portion of their foreign exchange receipts to republican authorities at the uniform exchange rate.

Republican authorities would, in turn, keep a portion of the foreign exchange, dividing the rest between central foreign exchange funds (for servicing Soviet debt) and local governments. Republican authorities would also receive foreign exchange directly for sales of fuels, raw materials, precious stones, and so on, in their territory. A portion of those receipts would be divided between the center and local governments, but the precise procedures for doing so were not specified.

The central government would manage foreign economic relations (under the close scrutiny of bodies composed of representatives of the constituent republics). The main policy tools would be those familiar in the West: licenses, tariffs, and exchange and interest rates.

The authors of the plan regarded the balance of payments crisis as too severe to allow the republics to borrow on an individual basis for balance-of-payments purposes, at least at the beginning. They recognized that such an arrangement would make foreign creditors nervous. The plan proposed a moratorium on new debt and recommended that the republics decide how to share in servicing the existing debt.[52] Any new borrowing for the union as a whole would require the agreement of all republics and would be serviced through contributions from all of them.[53] All foreign aid granted by the confederation would be jointly decided by the fifteen republics, and the plan foresaw—surely with justification—that aid flows would fall off sharply and thus would ease somewhat the debt-service burden.

Foreign investment in the Soviet economy would be encouraged, first by quickly introducing a full legal system consistent with world practice and by rapidly setting up a market. The intent of the plan was to immediately introduce a partially convertible ruble, and to move to a fully convertible ruble within the 500 days, with a view to stimulating foreign investment. In addition to inflows of private capital, the plan counted on credits and possibly aid from Western governments to ease the transition to markets.

From an economic point of view, the 500-Day Plan was the most realistic of any plan under discussion in 1990 in the USSR, and it outlined the full range of institutions necessary for a well-functioning market economy. Important from a political standpoint was the concept that the union would have to be reconstituted as part of the process of creating a market economy. The plan also made a logical case for addressing both economic and political issues through a single, large economic union, using one currency, with one price and financial system.

On the negative side were the speed with which the plan had been put together and the immense pressures for compromise that inevitably influenced its authors. Many of its other shortcomings had little to do with foreign economic relations and need only be mentioned here: the unrealistic and rather vague provisions for *razgorsudarstvlenie* and privatization; the ambitious plans to use sales of assets to help stabilize the economy; the ill-defined, and potentially inflationary, social safety

---

52. No serious effort was made to come up with a formula for this debt-service sharing, obviously a politically difficult task.

53. Individual republics could also borrow and would be totally responsible for servicing their debts.

124 OPEN FOR BUSINESS

net that was to be implemented in a one-republic, one-vote environment; and the assumption that the loose confederation could still take the difficult decisions required to stabilize the economy and move ahead with reform.[54] These flaws did not destroy the plan; it was a victim of political maneuverings outside the control of its authors. If political leaders had decided to proceed down the path outlined by the 500-Day Plan, that document would have been a reasonable place to start, but much more work would have been required to turn it into a schedule of action leading to a stable political and economic system.

Although the plan was not adopted, its potential implications for foreign economic relations are significant, since many of the ideas espoused by its authors have been, and will no doubt continue to be, reflected in other plans or in laws and regulations adopted by various successor states of the USSR.

The Currency Convertibility Issue

A currency is fully convertible when it can be exchanged freely, at a legal exchange rate, into another currency.[55] In that sweeping sense, only a handful of the world's most developed countries have convertible currencies. Most countries have certain restrictions on convertibility, usually on the capital account (that is, on using domestic currency to purchase foreign assets), the purpose being to encourage businessmen to reinvest in the local economy.[56]

Many more countries fulfill the conditions for "current account convertibility," which permits unrestricted exchange of the domestic for foreign currency to allow payment for imports or to allow exporters to the country to convert their receipts in the domestic currency into

54. For a more general discussion of the problems with the plan, see Hewett, "New Soviet Plan," pp. 151–65.

55. This section is based on the excellent discussion by John Williamson, "The Economic Opening of Eastern Europe," in John Williamson, ed., *Currency Convertibility in Eastern Europe* (Institute for International Economics, September, 1991).

56. Restrictions on capital convertibility include restrictions on profit repatriation, one of the most important variables influencing the climate for direct foreign investment in a country.

foreign currency. This is consistent with the definition of convertibility (so-called Article VIII convertibility) set forth by the International Monetary Fund (IMF). As of December 1990, 68 of the IMF's 152 members subscribed to the conditions for Article VIII convertibility.[57]

Whereas convertibility itself is simply a matter of a declaration, the economic conditions that allow a government to make that announcement with confidence are rather more complex. A government with no foreign exchange reserves and limited access to foreign credits may fear that a declaration of convertibility will cause the value of its currency to plunge and therefore ignite hyperinflation at home. The defense against that is a tight monetary policy; otherwise steep and continuous devaluations are indeed inevitable.

Leaders may also fear that removing restrictions on access to foreign exchange could lead to purchases of the "wrong" goods (say, luxury consumer goods rather than investment goods) or to uncontrolled exports of goods in demand on the home market. The only defense against that is a flexible price system which responds to supply and demand signals and thereby ensures that it is profitable to sell at home those goods in high demand. Such a system also ensures that would-be importers of investment goods have the wherewithal to compete with importers of luxury goods, assuming that high-value goods are being produced. A flexible price system is, in other words, a necessary condition to moving toward convertibility.

Convertibility, responsible fiscal and monetary policy, and a competitive market are therefore all interrelated. A government is flirting with economic disaster if it tries to move toward convertibility without simultaneously stabilizing the economy and moving toward a market system. Likewise, any effort to move toward a market system without stabilizing the economy or introducing convertibility will ultimately fail.

EARLIER PROPOSALS FOR A CONVERTIBLE RUBLE. Soviet officials realized for some time that a convertible ruble would pave the way for

---

57. *International Monetary Fund, 1990 Annual Report* (April 1990), p. 45; International Monetary Fund, Press Release 89/43, September 19, 1989; and International Monetary Fund, Press Release 90/23, May 22, 1991.

the integration of the Soviet economy into the global economy, by making it easier for Soviet businessmen to do business abroad and by encouraging foreign investment in the USSR. But what escaped them was the interconnection between stabilization, markets, and convertibility. As a result, they wasted time on some obviously implausible solutions to their problem.

In 1987, for example, authorities adopted the approach associated with the *Osnovnye polozheniia* and announced a plan to achieve ruble convertibility, beginning first with intra-CMEA trade and then moving to trade with capitalist countries.[58] Aside from the fact that the 1987 reform package fell far short of creating the preconditions for convertibility, it was strange to start off with intra-CMEA trade. The notion that a group of nations, all with inconvertible currencies, could go ahead and develop a convertible currency in their mutual trade was absurd on the face of it. The fact that it was official policy indicated just how little the leaders and the economists advising them knew about foreign economic relations.

Although no practical steps were taken to achieve convertibility, the goal continued to be proposed. In the far-reaching decree of December 1988 on foreign economic relations, Gosbank, the Foreign Trade Bank, and the Ministry of Finance were ordered to come up with concrete proposals for achieving partial convertibility of the ruble.[59] Apparently doing as they were told, they came up with a conservative appraisal cautioning that ruble convertibility would have to be preceded by a number of other measures aimed at a radical reform.

The Abalkin plan included a seemingly realistic, although somewhat sketchy, view of convertibility as the end result of a successful reform. It simply advised that the conditions necessary to achieve partial con-

---

58. "Osnovnye polozheniia"; and Philip Hanson, "Converting the Inconvertible Ruble," RL 281/87, July 16, 1987.

59. "Postanovlenie soveta ministrov SSSR: O dal'neishem razvitii vneshneekonomicheskoi deiatel'nosti gosudarstvennykh, kooperativnykh i inykh obshchestvennykh predpriiatii, ob''edinenii i organizatsii" (Decree of the Council of Ministers of the USSR: On the further development of foreign economic activities of state, cooperative, and other public enterprises, associations, and organizations), *Ekonomicheskaia gazeta*, no. 51 (December 1988), pp. 17–18.

vertibility should be in place by 1995. As discussed earlier, the plan also introduced the idea of currency auctions, which were expected to evolve into a currency market.

THE CONVERTIBLE RUBLE AND THE 500-DAY PLAN. The 500-Day Plan, which sought a much quicker transition to a market economy than the Abalkin plan, recommended what appeared to be complete ruble convertibility (possibly including convertibility on the capital account) as early January 1, 1992.[60] Such an early move to convertibility, at least on the current account, would not have been out of the question, as can be seen from the recent experience of Poland and Yugoslavia, both of which moved to current account convertibility in 1990. However, it is doubtful that the key preconditions for convertibility—a credible commitment to stabilizing the economy and to moving to a market—would have been met if the 500-Day Plan had been adopted.

The stabilization goal would have required a mechanism for coordinating fiscal and monetary policy among the newly sovereign republics. Yet the plan contained no details about how that would work. The taxing power of the center, for example, was weak, while its commitments—in defense, infrastructure, and key industries—remained great, suggesting a threat of large deficits. And although the intention was not to finance deficits at the republican levels, the republics would clearly have come under enormous pressure to spend large sums on the social safety net (indexation of incomes, unemployment insurance, welfare payments), yet would probably have been unable or unwilling to tax sufficiently to finance those expenditures. It strains credulity to think that, particularly at the beginning, the Interrepublican Economic Council could have withstood pressures to monetize republican deficits. For these reasons, financial controls would have been weak under the 500-Day Plan, and therefore a quick move to convertibility would have led to strong downward pressure on the currency.

The commitment to markets at the center of the 500-Day Plan looks less unequivocal in the details of the price system, which is the heart

60. *Perekhod k rynku*, pt. 1, pp. 117–18.

of any market economy. Although the intention was to free up whole-sale prices of manufactured goods, price controls were apparently scheduled to continue for some time on a wide range of consumer goods. More important, prices would be set for key primary products, fuels, and selected manufactured goods, on the basis of negotiations among the fifteen republics. These prices would most likely have remained below world market prices, and therefore the relative prices of energy-intensive goods (which would have been strongly influenced by these key prices) would have ended up systematically lower than world market prices. A move to convertibility in that context would have generated enormous outflows of goods, which would have led either to price changes or to administrative controls, most likely the latter. Without a much stronger commitment to using convertibility to import world market prices into the domestic economy, it would have been dangerous to move quickly to a convertible ruble.

The ruble convertibility advocated in the 500-Day Plan, like other aspects of the plan, was a move in the right direction. Still, it would have created problems if it had been implemented as proposed—although they would have been solvable. But because political considerations intervened, those problems did not arise.

The Fate of the 500-Day Plan

The presentation of the 500-Day Plan to USSR President Gorbachev and Russian Chairman Yeltsin set off a convoluted set of semipublic maneuverings that need not be recounted here in any detail.[61] Boris Yeltsin accepted the plan immediately, instructing Russian Prime Minister Ivan Silaev to take it to the Russian Supreme Soviet, which he did on September 5, 1990.[62] It was adopted on September 11 and was to go into effect on October 1, but implementation was postponed until May 1, then neglected.

61. See Hewett, "New Soviet Plan," pp. 148–51.
62. "Vtoraia sessiia Verkhovnogo Soveta RSFSR: Doklad I. S. Silaeva" (The second session of the Supreme Soviet of the RSFSR: Report of I. S. Silaev), *Sovetskaia Rossiia*, September 5, 1990, p. 4.

Mikhail Gorbachev, however, wavered and—after a period of in-credible confusion—pushed for a compromise between the 500-Day Plan and his own government's more conservative plan, the roots of which lay in Prime Minister Ryzhkov's May 1990 program that the Supreme Soviet had rejected. The result, the Presidential Plan, sub-mitted to and approved by the USSR Supreme Soviet in mid-October, pledged to stabilize the economy and to move toward a market economy more slowly than the 500-Day Plan recommended.[63] The confederal element of the 500-Day Plan was gone, as was the quick move toward privatization, price liberalization, or the other features that had distin-guished the 500-Day Plan from the simply rhetorical commitment to markets that the government had been espousing for some time.

The consequences of rejecting the 500-Day Plan continued to play out in the USSR for more than a year afterward. Mikhail Gorbachev tried to use his presidential powers to hold the union together—by force if necessary—and to create a "regulated" market economy. He worked to negotiate a new union treaty in place of the confederation, but many of the republics—the Baltics, Georgia, Moldova, Armenia, in particular—had lost interest in finding an accommodation. In place of the 500-Day Plan, Gorbachev sought to issue decrees introducing a market economy, but this was at best a questionable proposition if the center and periphery could not agree on who owned what and who controlled what aspects of economic activity.

Meanwhile, chaos was spreading and the economy sinking further into a sea of troubles. The time for large plans was past. The question was whether the turmoil of 1990–91 might inadvertently—to some extent despite the intentions of the central leadership—lead to a version of a market economy that would open to the global economy.

63. "Osnovnye napravleniia po stabilizatsii narodnogo khoziaistva i perekhodu k rynochnoi ekonomike" (Basic guidelines for the stabilization of the economy and the transition to a market economy), *Pravda*, October 18, 1990, pp. 1–4. See also Gor-bachev's speech, "Ob osnovnykh napravleniiakh po stabilizatsii narodnogo kho-ziaistva i perekhodu k rynochnoi ekonomike: Vystuplenie M. S. Gorbacheva na sessii Verkhovnogo Soveta SSR" (On the basic guidelines for the stabilization of the econ-omy and the transition to a market economy: Speech of M. S. Gorbachev to the session of the Supreme Soviet of the USSR), *Pravda*, October 20, 1990, pp. 1–2.

CHAPTER FIVE

The New Post-Soviet
Economies

UNDER MIKHAIL GORBACHEV the Soviet Union set out on an odyssey of economic and political reform that is still unfolding. Though far from finished, this transformation already ranks among the great developments of the twentieth century, along with the revolutions that made Russia into a communist state. One of the many purposes of Gorbachev's reforms was to open the country to the world economy, and he began the process with a devolution of power designed, as he stated frequently, to modernize the USSR and bring its economy and political system to a level commensurate with its immense military might. He sought to transform the Soviet Union into a superpower in every sense of that word.

The events of 1991, however, made it clear that the Soviet Union would not survive even the century in which it was created. Gorbachev's political reforms unleashed centrifugal pressures that ultimately tore apart the state Lenin and Stalin had constructed. His economic reforms, and the haphazard manner in which they were pursued, only made matters worse, providing yet another rationale for those separatist forces already determined to leave while the center was too weak to resist effectively. The failure of the three-day coup in August 1991, a last-ditch attempt to stop the dissolution of the union, in fact sealed its fate. What had been intended as a controlled process of reform and opening to the outside world spun out of control.

So far, the breakup of the old union has been, if not entirely orderly, at least relatively peaceful. Things are still unpredictable, of course. Risks remain, and it would be foolish not to be concerned about each and every step in the dismantling of a state with 30,000 nuclear weapons. Yet, without denying the dangers associated with current and future developments in the former USSR, it is important to consider the potential in what has been occurring. The old political and economic institutions, once a constant feature of the postwar scene, have crumbled, and new ones are emerging. Spearheaded by Russia, a new wave of ambitious reforms has been sweeping through the former USSR, and the first difficult and concrete steps have been taken.

Already it is no longer possible to speak of a single economy on the territory of the former Soviet Union. The various successor states are proceeding with economic reform at different rates and along different paths. Nevertheless, after decades of sharing the same political and economic fate, the former republics of the USSR are starting at similar points, and their reformed economies will have some common elements for a while. None of them has yet devised the democratic, free-market system that some had hoped, against formidable odds, would quickly emerge. But neither have they clung to the old, closed system, now being dismantled in each country. So far, the post-Soviet economies appear to be something in between, amorphous entities that are difficult to categorize or even to comprehend in anything but the vaguest outline. To ascertain how these former Soviet states will fit into the world economy in the coming years, it is important to try to flesh out this outline and to contemplate the possibilities it suggests.

This chapter begins with a brief discussion of what the central USSR leadership tried to do after the 500-Day Plan was rejected in the fall of 1990. It focuses primarily on the leadership's foreign economic policy but also touches on the general developments that affected the shape and consequences of that policy.

The second concern is to explain why the events of 1990 and 1991 diverged, sometimes considerably so, from what the government expected. This is where the republics and local authorities came into the picture. In many ways the opening of the economy went beyond the intentions of the central government, so that the leadership was repeatedly forced to try to catch up.

The third concern has to do with the dynamic between what the Soviet Union's successor governments are trying to do and what is happening on the ground. How are they intersecting and with what implications for the role of the new states in the global economy? And that, in turn, leads to a final question: how should the outside world regard these developments and relate to them?

From Shatalin to the Coup

The most informative, and in some ways prescient, source of information on the central government's approach to economic policy in 1991, including its foreign economic policy, is the May 1990 report of the Ryzhkov government to the USSR Supreme Soviet outlining its proposed stabilization and reform program.[1] The Supreme Soviet rejected this report, and by calling for a revised version, it directly provoked the debate of the summer of 1990 discussed in chapter 4. But the package was rejected mainly because of its macroeconomic stabilization and retail price components, not because of the market-oriented reform measures, which were basically accepted. And so, while the reform debates continued in the commissions, at the level of practical policy the Ryzhkov program actually began to be put into effect.

1. "Ob ekonomicheskom polozhenii strany i kontseptsii perekhoda k reguliruemoi rynochnoi ekonomike: Doklad Pravitel'stva SSSR na tret'iu sessiu Verkhovnogo Soveta SSSR" (On the economic situation of the country and the conception for the transition to a regulated market economy: Report of the government of the USSR to the third session of the Supreme Soviet of the USSR), Moscow, May 1990.

Creating the Market

In the late spring of 1990, Mikhail Gorbachev set out to implement the strategy laid out in the May report, using his powers as president to issue decrees or propose laws designed to move toward a "regulated" market economy. What followed was a rapid proliferation of laws or decrees in force, or in draft, covering many of the legal underpinnings of a market economy: a law legitimizing a wide range of property rights (including private property)[2]; a law sanctioning virtually all forms of enterprise[3]; a decree establishing an antitrust authority[4]; a draft of basic legal principles guiding destatization and privatization[5]; laws establishing a two-tiered banking system[6]; a draft of legal principles for legislation on labor markets[7]; decrees establishing a foreign exchange market[8]; a law on investment[9]; and laws on small business

2. "Zakon Soiuza Sovetskikh Sotsialisticheskikh Respublik: O sobstvennosti v SSSR" (Law of the Union of Soviet Socialist Republics: On property in the USSR), *Izvestiia*, May 10, 1990, 2.

3. "Zakon Soiuza Sovetskikh Sotsialisticheskikh Respublik: O predpriiatiakh v SSSR" (Law of the Union of Soviet Socialist Republics: On enterprises in the USSR), *Ekonomika i zhizn'* (Economics and life), no. 25 (June 1990), pp. 19–21.

4. "Postanovlenie Soveta Ministrov SSSR ot 16 avgusta 1990 g. No. 835: O merakh po demonopolizatsii narodnogo khoziaistva" (Decree of the Council of Ministers of the USSR of August 16, 1990, no. 835: On measures related to demonopolization of the economy), Supplement to *Ekonomika i zhizn'*, no. 38 (September 1990), pp. 2–3.

5. "Proekt: Osnovy zakonodatel'stva Soiuza SSR i respublik o razgosudarstvlenii sobstvennosti i privatizatsii predpriatii" (Draft: Foundations of legislation of the USSR on destatization of property and privatization of enterprises), *Ekonomika i zhizn'*, no. 7 (February 1991), pp. 18–19.

6. "Zakon Soiuza Sovetskikh Sotsialisticheskikh Respublik: O gosudarstvennom banke SSSR" (Law of the Union of Soviet Socialist Republics: On the state bank of the USSR), *Ekonomika i zhizn'*, no. 52 (December 1990), pp. 16–17; and "Zakon Soiuza Sovetskikh Sotsialisticheskikh Respublik: O bankakh i bankovskoi deiatel'-nosti" (Law of the Union of Soviet Socialist Republics: On banking and banking activity), ibid., pp. 17–18.

7. "Osnovy zakonodatel'stva Soiuza SSR i respublik o zaniatosti naseleniia" (The foundations of legislation of the Union of Soviet Socialist Republics on employment of the population), *Ekonomika i zhizn'*, no. 6 (February 1991), pp. 22–24.

8. "O merakh po formirovaniiu obshchesoiuznogo valiutnogo rynka" (On mea-

and on entrepreneurship (a radical law replacing the Law on Individual Labor Activity of 1985)[10].

In broad outline—though not in detail—all these central government decrees followed the strategy set forth in the 500-Day Plan, at least that part of the strategy relating to the creation of the market. That was only to be expected, since the plan and many of the decrees flowing from the Ryzhkov program were designed by the same people, working simultaneously on two different levels. As the 500-Day Plan staff put together their document, they were enjoined by Gorbachev and Boris Yeltsin to work with the government on practical policy, and in many areas, including foreign economic policy, they did so.[11] Where they differed from the leaders of the central government in strategy, and would differ in implementation, was on the speed of the

---

sures for the creation of an all-union foreign exchange market), USSR Council of Ministers Decree no. 776, August 4, 1990, *Sobranie postanovlenii Pravitel'stva Soiuza Sovetskikh Sotsialisticheskikh Respublik* (Collected decrees of the government of the Union of Soviet Socialist Republics), no. 19 (1990), pp. 428–29; and "Ukaz Prezidenta Soiuza Sovetskikh Sotsialisticheskikh Respublik: O vvedenii kommercheskogo kursa rublia k inostrannym valiutam i merakh po sozdaniiu obshchesoiuznogo valiutnogo rynka" (Decree of the president of the Union of Soviet Socialist Republics: On the introduction of a commercial rate of exchange for the ruble and measures for creating an all-union foreign exchange market), *Izvestiia*, October 26, 1990, p. 1.

9. "Osnovy zakonodatel'stva ob investitsionnoi deiatel'nosti v SSSR" (Foundations of legislation on investment activity in the USSR), December 10, 1990, *Vedomosti S"ezda narodnykh deputatov SSSR i Verkhovnogo Soveta SSSR* (Gazette of the Congress of People's Deputies of the USSR and the Supreme Soviet of the USSR), no. 51 (December 19, 1990), pp. 1343–53.

10. "O merakh po sozdaniiu i razvitiiu malykh predpriiatii" (On measures relating to the creation and development of small enterprises), USSR Council of Ministers Decree no. 790, August 8, 1990, *Sobranie Postanovlenii Pravitel'stva Soiuza Sovetskikh Sotsialisticheskikh Respublik*, no. 19 (1990), pp. 433–40; "Zakon Soiuza Sovetskikh Sotsialisticheskikh Respublik: Ob obshchikh nachalakh predprinimatel'stva grazhdan v SSSR" (Law of the Union of Soviet Socialist Republics: On the general principles of enterpreneurship of citizens in the USSR), *Izvestiia*, April 10, 1991, p. 2. Drafts on this latter law had circulated (under various names) since at least April of 1990.

11. The continuity of programs goes back even further, since in many cases the experts on the overlapping 500-Day and government policy teams had worked for the Abalkin Commission, if not on staff, then as consultants. See chap. 4, note 24.

move to a market economy and on the role of private ownership in that market system.

Foreign Economic Policy

Foreign economic strategy, too, unfolded in a stream of regulations, decrees, and laws that generally followed the path laid out by Ryzhkov in the spring of 1990.[12] Under that strategy, the union, not the republics, controlled foreign economic policy. Enterprises, and to some extent the republics, were allowed to retain more of their foreign exchange earnings than in the past, and the republics were to have more say over how the foreign exchange left over after debt servicing was to be spent. But all of this occurred according to laws and decrees issued by the central government.

Direct foreign trade rights, already scheduled to accrue to approximately 26,000 entities by January 1, 1991, were to spread to virtually all enterprises and other organizations in 1991.[13] For those enterprises that wished to use middlemen to purchase imports or sell their products abroad, the law encouraged that this be done competitively through various agencies, including foreign trade organizations, which were now to be "destatized" and turned into joint-stock trading companies operating on a profit-and-loss basis.[14]

12. "Ob ekonomicheskom polozhenii strany," pp. 52–56, outlines the foreign economic policy strategy of the Ryzhkov government.

13. Gosudarstvennyi komitet SSSR po statistike (State Committee of the USSR on Statistics), "Ekonomika SSSR v 1990 godu" (Economy of the USSR in 1990), *Ekonomika i zhizn'*, no. 5 (January 1991), pp. 9–13. In 1990 there were approximately 45,000 state-sector industrial enterprises in the USSR, 250,000 cooperatives, and 50,000 public (state and collective) farms. Theoretically, these and thousands of other smaller establishments would be able to engage in foreign trade in the future. In fact, of course, it was likely that in the USSR, as elsewhere, the overwhelming majority of enterprises would not engage directly in foreign trade. Data from Gosudarstvennyi komitet SSSR po statistike, *Narodnoe khoziaistvo SSSR v 1989 g.: Statisticheskii ezhegodnik* (National economy of the USSR in 1989: Statistical yearbook) (Moscow: Finansy i statistika, 1990), pp. 329, 501, 508; and "Ekonomika SSSR v 1990 godu," p. 9.

14. The September 3, 1990, antitrust legislation (see note 4), called for the "demonopolization" of foreign trade by shifting foreign trade organizations out of the

Foreign exchange earnings of all domestically owned enterprises (union, republican, local, private, and cooperative) were subject to several restrictions for 1991, although these were somewhat less arbitrary and had a more explicit rationale than before.[15] Forty percent of any enterprise's earnings had to be sold to Vneshekonombank (the Bank for Foreign Economic Relations) at the (extremely unfavorable) commercial rate for the explicit purpose of servicing the hard currency debt of the USSR.[16] The central government had originally wanted 60 percent, but the republics refused to go along.[17] Of the remaining 60 percent, exporters of fuel and raw materials were allowed to retain 20 to 40 percent and machinery and equipment producers up to a maximum of 70 percent.[18] The residual—after the initial 40 percent was taken off the top for debt servicing and the amount retained by the enterprise—also had to be sold at the commercial rate (10 percent to the

---

hands of the Ministry of Foreign Economic Relations and other ministries and converting them into broadly based trading houses.

15. The laws and regulations were provided in the Council of Ministers decree of August 4, 1990 ("O merakh po formirovaniiu obshchesoiuznogo valiutnogo rynka"); and the presidential decree of October 26, 1990 ("O vvdenii kommercheskogo kursa rublia"). See note 8. The details for 1991 can be found in "Postanovlenie Soveta Ministrov SSSR ot 8 dekabria 1990 g., No. 1253: O formirovanii valiutnykh fondov v 1991 godu" (Decree of the Council of Ministers of the USSR of December 8, 1990, no. 1253: On the formation of currency reserves in 1991), *Ekonomika i zhizn'*, no. 1 (January 1991), p. 25.

The sole exception here is "enterprises with the participation of foreign capital"—mainly joint ventures, but also under the new law presumably 100 percent foreign-owned entities. See "Ukaz Prezidenta Soiuza Sovetskikh Sotsialisticheskikh Respublik: Ob osobom poriadke izpol'aazovaniia valiutnykh resursov v 1991 godu" (Decree of the President of the Union of Soviet Socialist Republics: On the special procedure for the utilization of currency reserves in 1991), *Izvestiia*, November 3, 1990, p. 2.

16. The requirement to sell a sum of foreign currency at the commercial rate was tantamount to a tax of over 90 percent on that amount, since already by July 1990 the value of the ruble at the auction rate had dropped to about $1 = R20, while the commercial rate was about $1 = R1.8. See Yelena Deriabina, "Currency Auction Signals Ruble Rebound," *Commersant*, no. 44 (November 19, 1990), p. 6.

17. The original proposal is discussed in Mikhail Shvedov, "Sinking Competitive Spirits: Proposed Law Saps the Profits of Firms Exporting to Capitalist Countries," *Commersant*, no. 32 (August 20–27, 1990), p. 3.

18. "Postanavlenie Soveta Ministrov SSSR: O formirovanii valiutnykh fondov v 1991 godu."

republic in which the enterprise was located, and 90 percent to a newly formed Union-Republican Foreign Exchange Fund, which would henceforth set policy on debt servicing, new debt, and priorities for projects requesting centrally allocated foreign exchange).[19]

Those enterprises wishing to obtain foreign exchange in order to purchase imports would be able to go to a unionwide foreign exchange auction, which over time was to become a full-blown market. The exchange rate on this successor to the biweekly auctions of 1990 would float freely and be a much broader market than before, since more foreign exchange would remain in enterprise hands. Enterprises would be able to borrow foreign exchange not only from Vneshekonom-bank—as they had even before 1991—but also from commercial banks licensed by Gosbank to deal in foreign exchange, and even to borrow foreign exchange from foreign sources.[20]

The joint-venture legislation was quickly superseded by decrees authorizing direct foreign investment, including wholly owned foreign operations on Soviet soil. As of late 1990 it became legal under USSR law for foreign investors to buy into virtually any Soviet enterprise or to establish and operate their own enterprise. They would have the right to reinvest their rubles, or to repatriate them, according to procedures established in the new Soviet law.[21] The main restriction on foreign investors was that they could not buy land.

19. Again, this applied to all enterprises, including those set up by individual republics in an effort to earn foreign exchange for themselves. The only exception was for those enterprises involving foreign capital.

The Union-Republican Fund comprised the heads of government of the republics and the chairman of the State Foreign Economic Commission. It was chaired by the prime minister. See "Ukaz Prezidenta Soiuza Sovetskikh Sotsialisticheskikh Respublik: Ob osobom poriadke ispol'zovaniia valiutnykh resursov v 1991 godu."

20. The legislation on commercial foreign exchange operations can be found in "Zakon Soiuza Sovetskikh Sotsialisticheskikh Respublik: O gosudarstvennom banke SSSR"; and "Zakon Soiuza Sovetskikh Sotsialisticheskikh Respublik: O bankakh i bankovskoi deiatel'nosti."

21. The most important decree here was "Ukaz Prezidenta Soiuza Sovetskikh Sotsialisticheskikh Respublik: Ob inostrannykh investitsiakh v SSSR" (Decree of the President of the Union of Soviet Socialist Republics: On foreign investment in the USSR), *Izvestiia*, October 26, 1990, p. 1.

Wholesale pricing was to take the form of negotiated prices for many products, which meant that foreign trade prices would tend toward world prices, modified by the Soviets' own version of a "two-column" tariff system. As state orders began to lose their significance, a fairly open market would emerge for intermediate products.

What Kind of Market?

These regulations, decrees, and laws brought the first real glimpse of a market economy to the USSR in 1990. The banking system, foreign exchange markets, new laws encouraging direct foreign investment, procedures for destatization and privatization—all were to be implemented basically as recommended in the 500-Day Plan. On paper, the 500-Day Plan, at least the market side of it, was coming alive.

But by early 1991, regulations, decrees, and laws mattered less in the USSR than they had before—and they had never mattered as much as bureaucrats thought they should. Part of the problem was that the center and the republics were engaged in a "battle of laws" and were issuing numerous conflicting decrees that in effect left enterprises and local authorities to act on their own account. In addition, the sometimes inept, never inspired economic policy of the central government had so undermined popular confidence in central leaders that their decrees were being taken less seriously than they had been even a few years before.

A Voluntary or Mandatory Union?

The 500-Day Plan had called for a voluntary union among the fifteen republics. It even allowed for the possibility that some republics would not join but would request observer status. The authors of the plan had done their best to devise a scheme that would entice all the republics to join. They even consulted with representatives of virtually all the republics to make sure the framework had universal appeal.

Although Mikhail Gorbachev sent varying signals after the summer of 1990, his basic message was unmistakable: he would simply not permit the union to break apart. Thus, even though procedures for secession had been announced in the spring of 1990, they were so onerous that it was felt no republic would want to follow through with them.[22]

At the same time, Gorbachev made an effort to capture the spirit of the confederal side of the 500-Day Plan without actually conceding that sovereignty rested solely in the republics and not in the center. A fast-paced set of changes introduced in November 1990, along with a new draft union treaty, restructured the USSR government to give interrepublican bodies a greater advisory and decisionmaking role. The Presidential Council, a consultative body created by Gorbachev in March 1990, was disbanded. In its place, the Federation Council—composed of the heads of each of the union and autonomous republics and the president and vice president of the union (the latter a newly created post)—was given broad powers to coordinate policy at the all-union level. The draft union treaty itself granted the republics broad powers establishing the primacy of their laws over union laws in all areas except defense, foreign policy, and the regulation of foreign economic activity.[23]

This attempt to placate the republics did not have the desired effect, certainly not for the Baltic states, Georgia, or even Russia. If anything, it hardened their opposition to the new centrally issued laws and decrees, even if those laws were well designed. When Gorbachev rejected the confederal proposal in the 500-Day Plan, the divisions between the center and the republics grew even more pronounced. Thenceforth,

---

22. "Zakon Soiuza Sovetskikh Sotsialisticheskikh Respublik: O razgranichenii polnomochii mezhdu Soiuzom SSR i sub"ektami federatsii" (Law of the Union of Soviet Socialist Republics: On delineation of powers between the Union of Soviet Socialist Republics and the subjects of the federation), *Izvestiia*, May 3, 1990, pp. 1–2.

23. The new governmental structure was described in the draft union treaty, "Proekt: Soiuznyi dogovor" (Draft: The union treaty), *Izvestiia*, November 24, 1990, pp. 1–2. Although the treaty itself was never approved, the government structure was approved by the Supreme Soviet on December 5, 1990. See S. Chugayev, "Predlozheniia Prezidenta SSSR podderzhany" (Proposals of the President of the USSR accepted), *Izvestiia*, December 5, 1990, pp. 1–2.

every law issued by the center was automatically taken as a challenge to republican authority. By October 1990 the conflict had become so acrimonious that Mikhail Gorbachev had to ask the USSR Supreme Soviet to pass a law ordering republics to obey union laws in areas in which the union had declared itself to be sovereign.[24]

In response, the Baltic states, led by a militant Lithuania, decided to withdraw entirely from negotiations over the union. They openly stated that they no longer regarded themselves as part of the union—consequently, they saw no need to secede formally and certainly had no interest in participating in a federal structure imposed on them by Moscow. Their dissent had tragic repercussions: in January 1991 fourteen Lithuanian civilians were killed in attacks by Soviet forces.

Although the Baltic states were an extreme case within the USSR, they were symbolic of the general problem. The architects of the 500-Day Plan had been acutely aware that the government could not hope to take the difficult measures necessary to launch a market economy without the full support of the republics. Yet there was Gorbachev trying to introduce a market while virtually at war with the republics. His approach was, in effect, the 500-Day Plan on one leg—the market leg—without the confederal, or political, leg to allow it to stand on its own.

Whether the 500-Day Plan would have succeeded in forging a new union can never be known. What is clear is that after Gorbachev rejected the plan he was never able to gain the trust of the republics. Even his apparent success in securing the so-called 9 + 1 Agreement in April 1991, when nine of the fifteen republics of the USSR pledged to sign a union treaty, proved to be a Pyrrhic victory. To obtain their cooperation, Gorbachev was forced to recognize the republics as sovereign states.

24. "Zakon Soiuza Sovetskikh Sotsialisticheskikh Respublik: Ob obespechenii deistviia zakonov i inykh aktov zakonodatel'stva soiuza SSR" (Law of the Union of Soviet Socialist Republics: On guaranteeing the force of laws and other legislative acts of the Union of Soviet Socialist Republics), *Izvestiia*, October 26, 1990, p. 3.

The Issue of Confidence

Markets thrive in an environment of confidence—confidence that the rules of the game are well known, stable, and sure to be enforced, and that there is no doubt about who owns what or who regulates what kind of economic activity. The environment in the USSR in 1991 inspired confidence in none of these areas.

The battle of laws had made it even less clear who owned or controlled what. Already by September 1990 most republics had declared that their laws superseded Soviet laws in all areas, not just in those Gorbachev had outlined.[25] There was a Russian law on banks and a union law on banks, a Russian law on foreign investment and a union law on foreign investment, a Russian law on land reform and a union law on land reform, and so on for other areas of the economy and for other republics.

Moreover, there was no indication that private investment, the all-important component of a market economy, would be stimulated and would thus give rise to new enterprises, and even new industries. Again, that required some confidence that the government would implement policies conducive to profitmaking and that it would not confiscate those profits. On both counts the Soviet government under Gorbachev earned low marks.

Throughout the winter and spring of 1991 the Soviet government showed no sign of fulfilling its pledge to stabilize the economy by reducing the budget deficit. Efforts to raise retail prices to levels that would not require subsidies—which were at the heart of the budget deficit—met with enormous resistance and revealed just how weak the government was. In April the new government of Prime Minister

---

25. By August 25, 1990, thirteen of the fifteen republics of the USSR had adopted declarations of sovereignty or independence. The final two—Kazakhstan and Kirgizia—followed by November 1. All these declarations in one way or another asserted supremacy of republican over all-union laws, although not all republics had made the changes to give the declarations force of law. See Ann Sheehy, "Fact Sheet on Declarations of Sovereignty," RFE/RL, *Report on the USSR*, November 9, 1990, pp. 23–25.

Valentin Pavlov undertook a halfway measure of price reform.[26] Although this could in no way be considered true price liberalization, it caused enough pain to antagonize the population. Following on the heels of Pavlov's bungled effort in January to eliminate the so-called ruble overhang by confiscating currency, the April price increases further undermined whatever confidence the population still had in the new government.[27]

In the meantime, the failure to stabilize the ruble discouraged any but the shortest-term investments and encouraged speculation in dollars. Official concern over this and other perceived speculative activity had already led Gorbachev in early 1991 to authorize the use of the KGB to investigate—without a warrant—any business (including joint ventures) suspected of "crimes in the economic sphere."[28] The vague, seemingly unbounded nature of the threat, accompanied by increasing signs of a general shift to the right on other economic issues, could only add to the uncertainty surrounding current or would-be small businessmen in the USSR.

These concerns were particularly acute for the foreign business

26. Pavlov, who had served as Gorbachev's finance minister since 1989, succeeded Nikolai Ryzhkov as prime minister in January 1991. Ryzhkov had suffered a heart attack in late December.

27. The currency reform, which took place on January 22, 1991, declared all existing 50 and 100 ruble notes invalid. A small percentage of the notes could be exchanged for new currency. Government spokesmen had initially claimed that the confiscation would remove up to 38 billion "excess" rubles from circulation. See Keith Bush, "Gorbachev's First Currency Reform," *Report on the USSR*, no. 5 (February 1, 1991), pp. 25–26. It was later admitted that the net decrease had actually been less than 7 billion rubles, or barely more than 1 percent of the total money supply at the time. See Michael Alexeev, Clifford Gaddy, and Jim Leitzel, "An Economic Analysis of the Ruble Overhang," *Communist Economies and Economic Transformation*, no. 4 (1991), pp. 467–79.

28. Quentin Peel, "KGB Given Tough New Powers in Economic Crackdown," *Financial Times*, January 28, 1991, p. 6; and "Ukaz Prezidenta Soiuza Sovetskikh Sotsialisticheskikh Respublik: O merakh po obespecheniiu bor'by s ekonomicheskim sabotazhem i drugimi prestupleniiami v sfere ekonomiki" (Decree of the President of the Union of Soviet Socialist Republics: On measures for ensuring the struggle against economic sabotage and other crimes in the sphere of the economy), *Izvestiia*, January 28, 1991, p. 1.

community, already uneasy about the apparent flagging support for radical reform in the USSR. Any foreign investor had to balance the possibilities presented by the new laws on foreign investment against the tone set by the Soviet government, especially toward foreign investors. In late 1990 and early 1991 that tone turned markedly negative when KGB Chairman Vladimir Kriuchkov alluded to foreign plots to foist tainted grain on the USSR, and Prime Minister Pavlov explained his bungled currency reform in part as an effort to thwart an international conspiracy to flood the Soviet Union with rubles, hyperinflate the economy, and buy up choice Soviet property. Although this overtly xenophobic tone was moderated in the spring of 1991, it returned with increased strength in June and July.[29]

Ultimately, economic confidence depends on whether a nation's leadership is truly committed to introducing markets in the sense that businessmen—even Soviet businessmen—understand them. Clearly, men like Pavlov and Kriuchkov did little to instill faith that the Soviet leadership believed in markets. More serious, it seemed that Gorbachev himself could never fully endorse the idea of the market or even provide the same tone of support that had been evident in the 500-Day Plan, which had been in favor of a relatively free-wheeling, competitive market economy. Instead, Gorbachev continued to appear basically distrustful of markets.

With his government pursuing—in its best moments—a "go slow" approach to the market, the politically beleaguered Gorbachev increasingly focused his own attention in the spring and summer of 1991 on the union. Meanwhile, in the person of Russian leader Boris Yeltsin, the market idea was finding a champion who was also gaining in popular support.

29. Kriuchkov's allegations were first made in a televised speech to the Soviet parliament on December 22, 1990. See RFE/RL, *Report on the USSR*, no. 1 (January 4, 1991), p. 58. Pavlov revealed the alleged bankers' plot in "V. S. Pavlov: 'Budem realistami' " (V. S. Pavlov: "We will be realists"), *Trud*, February 12, 1991. For public statements in June by Pavlov and Kriuchkov alleging foreign conspiracies against Russia, see RFE/RL, *Report on the USSR*, no. 24 (June 14, 1991), p. 35, and no. 27 (July 5, 1991), p. 27.

Through Chaos to the Market

To obtain pledges from the republics to sign the April 1991 agreement on a new form for the union, Gorbachev had not only acknowledged the principle of republican sovereignty but had also made a decisive concession to Yeltsin, his chief political rival. As part of their pre-agreement maneuvering, Gorbachev had dropped his opposition to Yeltsin's effort to stand for direct election as president of Russia.

For Yeltsin, the landslide victory of June 12 was a mandate to abandon the regulated market model and proceed with reforms like those outlined in the 500-Day Plan. In his rivalry with Gorbachev, Yeltsin had defined himself as the unconditional advocate of a free-market economy. When the events of August thrust him into the position of sole leader of Russia and temporarily of the union, Yeltsin found the road to the market completely open. In the final weeks of the USSR, Yeltsin, drawing along with him the leaders of the other republics of the de facto independent states, brought economic reform to the fore.

Whereas at the end of 1990 it had seemed merely very likely that a market would emerge in the USSR, by the fall of 1991 it was nearly inevitable. The difference now was there would be not one market but a multiplicity of markets. The fundamental question thus became, what sort of markets would they be? In thinking about what the markets in the post-Soviet states will look like, one must rely primarily on imagination, since their nature is only implicit in the current laws and the chaos surrounding them.

Political Assumptions

Under Gorbachev, one of the critical factors affecting the shape of the new market had been the battle between the republics and the center over the control of the economy, and of the political system. That struggle was not fully resolved in the aftermath of the August 1991 coup, but it was radically redefined. Although the republics still disagree on many points in the framework of their new association—the

Commonwealth of Independent States (CIS), formed in December 1991— these are disagreements among partners of (at least formally) equal status. No longer do the nature and pace of economic reform depend on a center; they are up to each separate national leadership.

The breakup of the old Soviet Union is not a guarantee of reform in all the successor states. Certainly, some republics may resist, although in just the short time since August 1991 it has become unthinkable that there could be a return to the status quo of, say, 1980 or earlier. However convoluted the course of political and economic liberalization in the former USSR, the events of the past seven years have so profoundly touched people and institutions there that it is difficult to conceive of a leadership sufficiently brutal, and a brutality sufficiently successful, to forcibly impose a totalitarian regime in large nations such as Russia, Ukraine, or Belarus. *Glasnost'* and *perestroika* have some of the characteristics of one-way membranes: no matter how much some leaders and even many ordinary citizens may wish to go back, a return would most likely be blocked by what has already happened.

For the Soviet successor states as a group, there may eventually be some movement toward a new form of political and economic integration. This is not, however, the most probable course of events in the short term. The current CIS structures do not appear to be entering into a more solid union, but to be sinking further into dissolution and a prolonged period of unspoken, and uneasy, truce among the former republics. Instead of signing formal documents in public ceremonies, the new nations will more than likely develop a rather loose and incomplete understanding as the result of individual deals on specific issues. As for the economic disputes between Russia and the other republics—concerning control over financial and other assets, division of the debt (domestic and foreign), and so on—they will no doubt remain for some time to come, and solutions will probably take the form of compromises on pragmatic grounds.

Because of the chaotic diversity of the new post-Soviet reality, no single economic model will be sought in the uneasy negotiations among the former republics. The unavoidable effects of each nation's—most notably Russia's—economic policies on the others will certainly make for acrimonious relations as the republics engage in a new battle of laws, this time across national boundaries.

Outlines of the Emerging Market

As events have already shown, relations among the former Soviet republics are going to present acute problems for their economies. Yet the political environment will generally be favorable to a market-type system over the long term. The breakup of the union was in part merely one element of the basic trend toward decentralization throughout the *perestroika* era, and, as is well known, decentralization is a prerequisite to creating markets. The overall process of decentralization has been an interesting mix of centrally directed decentralization, and decentralization by default, when political conditions created a vacuum at the top and individual enterprises or localities simply took matters into their own hands. The advantage of individual enterprises in the battle of decrees is that they have been able to play one side off against the other, thereby acquiring more control over their own affairs.

Governments at all levels, if only out of the inertia of their old and still influential bureaucracies, will surely try to regulate this market. But few are likely to feel that they have more than a loose grip on the system.

Given this background, the new economies will no doubt be dominated for some time to come by large enterprises. Formally, they may remain "state" enterprises, but in fact they will be heavily controlled by their managers, who have been emerging as the de facto owners of the large state enterprises. Eventually most of the large enterprises will be destatized and even privatized, but whatever their formal title, enterprises will in fact be run by their managers.

The continued dominance of the large enterprises is a logical outgrowth of their market power and of their strong connections with the government bureaucracy and with the increasingly influential big banks. In the new world, where obligatory plans are displaced by a mass of shifting regulations, the large enterprises will be able to negotiate changes that will ensure that the environment is one in which they can manage to operate. This will be especially true of enterprises that dominate the local economy, since local politicians have come to realize that in the absence of central government support and investment funds, the large enterprises in their own area will be their only source of financial support. A second category of potentially successful enterprises in the new environment will be those traditionally under the defense ministries. For many of them, their former access to technology and skilled labor may make them somewhat more competitive on world markets than nondefense enterprises.

The de facto property rights of the managers will depend on their expertise and connections. Because the Communist party emphasized expertise in its choice of enterprise managers, an experienced and capable managerial corps is available that will certainly survive the transition to a market, at least its first phase. In the future, these managers may formally report to shareholders, including foreign shareholders. But in the chaotic post-Soviet environment of the 1990s, they will hold the upper hand against interfering outsiders who think it is easy to survive, let alone thrive, in that system.

At the other end of the spectrum, small enterprises will surely find a niche in the interstices left by the industrial behemoths. Whether in services, the production of small consumer goods, or the supply of some components to industry, the post-Soviet economies can draw on a substantial legacy of small private enterprise left by the Gorbachev reforms. By mid-1991 the USSR already had 260,000 private cooperatives employing about 4.5 million people on a full-time basis (and nearly 2 million part-time). Another half million citizens were self-employed in so-called individual labor activity. Together, these two new categories of legal private employment accounted for nearly 4 percent of the 130-million-person active labor force—a modest figure, perhaps, but up from virtually zero four years earlier.[30]

All of this occurred in an environment generally hostile to small business. That unfriendliness will most likely continue in many republics and regions. At best, small businessmen can count on an inconsistent view of their efforts to make a profit, and at times some

30. Gosudarstvennyi Komitet SSSR po statistike, "Ekonomika SSSR v 1990 godu," p. 9.

of them may even be singled out for being too profitable. But the potential profits will be huge, and the continuing high rates of inflation will induce ever larger numbers of workers in wage-constrained state enterprises to moonlight in the private sector or even move over entirely to small business ventures.

However, this market is not likely to invite a significant degree of competition. The old Soviet industrial structure inherited by the successor states was so highly concentrated that serious competition between two or more producers is not only physically unlikely, but in many cases impossible. In machine building, one-third of the USSR's important products were manufactured by only one enterprise, and another third by only two producers. According to estimates from Gossnab (the USSR State Committee for Material-Technical Supply), 80 percent of the volume of output in machine building in a recent year was manufactured by monopolists.[31] In general, high concentration is the norm, as a result of a conscious policy by Soviet leaders to merge industrial plants into a few large unions in the elusive search for economies of scale.

Although the economic reform laws on the books of the former USSR proclaim free entry, and various forms of antitrust regulations theoretically protect that right, in reality large firms will hold on to their markets, to the detriment of consumers and workers. As already mentioned, large firms will have the necessary connections with the large (formerly state-owned) banks. They will also be in a position to attract foreign investors, who will be looking for partners that dominate the domestic market and that are experienced in international markets. And since the republics and localities will look to them as major employers and spenders, they will have the political pull required to shape policy to their advantage. What will emerge will basically be a

31. For a more detailed discussion of these and other indications of the degree of economic concentration in Soviet industry, see Heidi Kroll, Monopoly and Transition to the Market," *Soviet Economy*, no. 2 (April–June, 1991), pp. 143–74. But see also Oleh Havrylyshyn and John Williamson, *From Soviet Disunion to Eastern Economic Community?* (Washington: Institute for International Economics, 1991), pp. 21–22, for arguments on why actual monopolization may not be as severe a problem as it is often thought to be.

two-tiered economy with a highly concentrated industrial core and very little competition, and a much smaller, marginal, market system on the fringes.

Finally, this is likely to be an inflationary economy. In the past, neither the union nor the republican governments were strong enough to impose a tight money policy, something that seems destined to elude the post-Soviet governments as well. The large enterprises, and their local government allies, will tend to prefer inflation to tight money, given their ability to pass cost increases on to consumers.

The picture painted here is not necessarily a market economy of the sort prevalent in Western Europe or the United States. If it has a counterpart, it may be in the economies of the Republic of Korea, Chile, or Taiwan. But in view of the multinational nature of the former Soviet republics and the still uncertain commitment of the central government bureaucracies (as opposed in some cases to the elected legislative and executive figures) to genuine market-type processes, the system will continue to be a very special case.

Open for Business?

The role of foreign trade, and of foreign economic relations in general, is as yet unclear in the new systems. So far the post-Soviet governments have continued and even intensified the Gorbachev regime's broad effort to achieve acceptance in the world economic community and to find markets for their exports. Laws allowing 100 percent foreign-owned firms to operate on their soil, the opening of the foreign exchange market, and the successful efforts to join the International Monetary Fund and the World Bank are but a few indicators of the desire of leaders of all the post-Soviet nations to finish what Mikhail Gorbachev began in 1986–87.

The fate of the new leaders' intentions will depend, first, on whether Western businesses and banks decide to wait out this transition period until the course of political and economic developments in the new nations becomes clear. Second, the leaders will find Western governments becoming more discriminating in their willingness to provide assistance. Up until now, the ex-Soviet states have collectively enjoyed the goodwill of people and governments in the West. As the republics begin to differentiate themselves through independently chosen policies, they will in turn be treated more selectively by the outside world. That is to say, those governments that retain significant controls on economic and political activity can expect greater penalties—in the form of less aid.

The Economics of the Post-Soviet Union

How these new post-Soviet economies will perform is far from clear, since not even the full outline of their systems is yet apparent. But if the conjectures offered above are close to the mark, then many people, both at home and abroad, will be disappointed not only by the economies' macroeconomic results but also by their export performance.

For a number of reasons large enterprises are likely to have a fairly easy time making money in their new economies. They begin with tremendous power in their markets. Moreover, their connections with the large banks ensure a decent chance at finance, when needed. Similarly good connections with national and local government officials will allow them to make special deals on taxes, and possibly even to retain their subsidies. And although the market will be formally open to imports, in fact it will most likely remain highly protected, as a result not so much of the tariff system as of a depressed exchange rate and informal import controls.

There will be no compelling reasons for large enterprises to go through the extraordinary efforts necessary to develop markets abroad for their manufactured goods. Some enterprises may do so, lured by the potential profits to be gained from continued cheap domestic energy and raw materials, but most are likely to focus primarily on the domestic market. They will look outside only if money grows tight and the various levels of government in Russia and the other nations are tough on subsidies. In those circumstances large enterprises would be forced to export or go under, and some of them would probably make a credible showing in world markets. But so far the preferred path seems to be to ally with local governments—using the argument of protecting jobs—to receive continued subsidies. The "battle of laws" transferred down to the subrepublican level seems destined to make it easy for enterprises to gain special favors during this chaotic period, which would preclude a really tough stand on subsidies or tax forgiveness.

Small enterprises may be more interested in exports, but they will not have the experience or the connections to make much headway here. The financial system is unlikely to open up and provide capital to small entrepreneurs, who are already finding foreign exchange almost totally in the control of the government and large business. Small business will have trouble breaking into this system until, and if, the entire set of institutions handling financial intermediation opens up.

As flawed as it is, this system is unquestionably an improvement over the old one. At least it links the ability of enterprises to obtain finance and foreign exchange, however loosely, to their performance. In the past foreign exchange was allocated entirely within the bureaucracy, the final distribution being the outcome of protracted, closed bureaucratic negotiations. Now capital and foreign exchange allocation will come out into the open, although perhaps not very far. The important determinants will still be size of enterprise and level of performance on the protected domestic market—in other words, the export performance of manufactured goods will continue to be poor.

If it proves possible, with help from foreign capital, to sustain the exports of raw materials and fuels, then the system will not starve for foreign exchange. But the freer access to foreign exchange will unveil the heretofore suppressed demand for imports that will lead to continuous, and enormous, pressures on the balance of payments.

Foreign Investors and the New Systems

It will be easier than it has been in the past to invest in the territory of the former Soviet Union, and—at least according to the law—to repatriate profits. Of course, foreign investors will remain most interested in selling their products to consumers inside the former USSR. And the new systems will permit that, at least in theory. The big enterprises will be by far the most appealing partners because of their political connections and their awesome position in domestic markets. Even so, small enterprises will not lose out entirely in the search for foreign partners, since they will be much more flexible and eager to work hard than most of the large enterprises.

In large part, the future role of the post-Soviet economies in the global economy will depend on how governments resolve the "battle of laws" and what tone they set as the legal environment begins to clarify itself. Right now Western businessmen are understandably nervous about systems in which virtually all productive capital remains nationalized; yet it is not clear precisely which government authority holds title, and therefore who will be in charge of the generally agreed upon commitment to privatize, or at least destatize, property. A further source of concern is the fact that it is unclear whose law applies in these systems, or whether there is applicable law for that matter.

As long as this situation continues, direct investment is unlikely to rise above the modest flow of recent years. Even some of the large projects that obviously hold enormous benefit for the former USSR—such as the agreements with several major oil companies to push ahead with the development of oil fields using advanced technology—will remain on hold as long as the companies are unsure who on the ex-Soviet side can sign and enforce the contact.

But here, as elsewhere, it is likely that over time the various warring factions within and among the new nations will work out truces of sorts, which will be sufficiently clear and believable to stimulate a flow of foreign capital. The first agreements will probably emerge in fuels, where the stakes are high—these were the backbone of the USSR's exports and will be for several of the new nations as well—and the solution is fairly simple. The most important issue here will be not which governmental authority "owns" the oil but rather how to divide the flow of dollars coming in after these deposits are exploited. Once that is resolved—and it is an imminently resolvable issue—the contracts will follow fairly easily.

Contracts for direct foreign investment to develop manufactured goods will be longer in coming to the new post-Soviet economies, although even now there are some interesting possibilities. If foreigners are indeed going to be allowed to convert rubles back into hard currency and escape punitive duties, then it may well pay for a foreign investor to operate a "screwdriver" operation (for example, simple assembly of a product) to get around the tariffs and obtain direct access to the distribution system. It would make sense to manufacture products that will sell for ruble-dollar ratios well in excess of the going auction rate, and if the authorities (and enterprises) of Russia or other successor nations allow it, such activity would inject a welcome supply of new goods, and some competition, into the system. Gradually these simple assembly operations could in some cases switch to domestic sourcing, which would probably increase profits, at least until the economy was strengthened and the exchange rate along with it (which could be some time off).

The critical factor here will be the national authorities of the new states, who will be anxious for exports (and the foreign exchange they bring) and who will tend to place obstacles in the way of any foreign investor who seeks only to develop the domestic market. There will likely be enough regulations in this market to make it difficult for any investor to set up operations (and get all the necessary bureaucratic clearances) unless he promises some form of export revenues. If that proves to be the case, then the flow of capital will be more limited than it would otherwise have to be. This is one area in which local authorities who have a say in investment in their territory could stimulate the inflow of foreign capital. They would no doubt be interested in expanding the supply of relatively high-quality, Western-type consumer goods, even if the immediate result was not exports and foreign currency revenues.

Western Governments and the Post-Soviet Economies

The world has an enormous vested interest in a peaceful and successful transition to political and economic pluralism in the nations of the former USSR. Not only would this guarantee the continuation of the "new thinking" that has so transformed the global political landscape in the past few years, but more prosperous post-Soviet economies would probably be more stable neighbors for Europe and for Asia.

Western influence over the outcome of this great drama is relatively modest. We may be able, on the margin, to make a difference here or there, but in the main this is an internally driven process that we will watch from the sidelines.

Whatever influence we do have will be channeled through the economy. The advice we give and the conditions placed on public and private financial support will, in the end, have some effect on the shape of the new economic system. We must therefore think carefully about what we would like to do, and how to accomplish it.

A Potential for Marginal Leverage

During most of the "Soviet" phase of economic reform before 1992, the role of Western governments was limited primarily to offering abundant advice and encouragement for what many saw as a rapid move to a market economy. It was only in 1990, in response to the collapse of the Eastern European empire and the emerging commitment in the Soviet leadership to a market economy, that government-sponsored credits began to flow in significant amounts. By the end of 1990, the USSR had secured credit commitments of approximately $17 billion, mostly for 1991, and mostly from Europe.[32] As of early 1992, that figure had risen to more than $80 billion.[33]

These government-guaranteed loans have become critical to future financing of the post-Soviet development process. By the middle of 1990, the failure to repay some $5 billion in interest and principal on earlier loans and the confusion associated with repaying those credits had so destroyed the Soviet credit rating that Soviet bankers were encountering difficulties in even refinancing short-term credits, here-

32. International Monetary Fund, International Bank for Reconstruction and Development, Organization for Economic Cooperation and Development, and the European Bank for Reconstruction and Development, *The Economy of the USSR: A Study Undertaken in Response to a Request by the Houston Summit, Summary and Recommendations* (Washington, 1990), p. 15.

33. Institute of International Finance, *USSR/CIS Country Report* (February 7, 1992), p. 17.

tofore virtually automatic for a creditor of the USSR's standing.[34] By
September 1990 Deutsche Bank—one of the USSR's principal sources
of credit—was refusing to finance loans with a 95 percent government
guarantee, insisting instead on a 100 percent guarantee.[35] Until this
inherited balance-of-payments situation is brought under control, which
will require considerable progress in stabilizing the new economies
and moving ahead with the reforms, government-guaranteed credits
will be the only source of significant new capital for the former USSR.

Leverage to Do What?

In view of the circumstances, the governments of the successor
states will probably be willing to adjust their policies to attract further
capital, and as their economic plight worsens, Western leverage will
increase. As the Russian case has already demonstrated, the adjustments can be quite large, going beyond the economic sphere to overtly
political action. Here the West must proceed with caution, however.
There are limits to the political conditions that can be imposed; any
heavy resort to such pressure (explicitly asking for a limit on defense
expenditures, for example) may produce a far stronger xenophobic
reaction than the rather mild manifestations seen so far. But if the
conditions are clearly related to economics, and if they are presented
with due consideration for diplomatic complexities, they can have a
salutory effect.

As the new economies evolve in the former USSR, Western governments ought to stay involved in the process, both through international organizations and bilaterally. Whatever credits they offer should
be targeted to specific projects and recipients. Their general goal should
be to foster competition and therefore to shore up those elements of
the system—small- and medium-size business, independent banks, and
so on—that would contribute to that goal. It makes no sense whatsoever
to give general-purpose, untied loans to the central governments; but

---

34. Craig Forman, "Soviet Officials Scour Europe in Search of New Loans but
Find Cold Welcome," *Wall Street Journal*, June 15, 1990, p. A2.

35. David Marsh and Katharine Campbell, "Deutsche Bank Downgrades Soviet
Rating," *Financial Times*, January 15, 1991, p. 6.

it does make good sense to get funds into the hands of small businesses starved for capital and foreign exchange.

By supporting the development of these new entrants into the post-Soviet markets, Western credits would stimulate the competition needed to improve long-term economic performance and at the same time would help promote diversity in the system. It is unclear whether a great deal of lending needs to go to republican or local governments. To the extent that investment is needed for communications, roads, sewage, and other infrastructure, foreign capital should go to projects that would attract additional foreign investment, and the recipient should be the level of government that is in charge of the desired infrastructure component. If the recipients are economic units that are typically private in Western countries, an effort might be made to focus on joint-venture banks or other institutions operating independently of any government—national or local.

It will be a challenge for Western governments to define a policy focused on supporting competition and openness in the post-Soviet economies, and to protect that policy from the vagaries of the general political relationship. Some difficulties are bound to arise in the West's relations with the successor states of the Soviet Union, individually or collectively—whether they touch on human rights, nuclear and conventional arms negotiations, territorial disputes, or other areas. When they do, loan packages and other aspects of the economic relationship will be among the first casualties, because they are one of the few potential vehicles for registering Western disapproval. Moreover, even the best-intentioned governments in this region will not always pursue the tough economic policies needed to stabilize the economies of these new states.

If, however, Western governments can manage to structure a package—and build a political consensus for it—that reinforces progressive forces in the emerging market systems, then it just might be possible to ride out the inevitable economic and political ups and downs of the coming decade. Should that prove to be the case, we will have moved closer, in however small a degree, to the creation of viable post-Soviet economies that are capable not only of meeting the needs of their own populations but also of becoming a strong force in the global economy.

Index

157

162 OPEN FOR BUSINESS

tion of, 40; Yeltsin's move toward, 90, 116, 119, 143, 144
Marrese, Michael, 50n, 51n
Marsh, David, 155n
Masliukov, Yuri, 106n
Mikhailov, A. Iu., 120n
Military Industrial Commission, 31
Ministry of Foreign Affairs, 35
Ministry of Foreign Economic Relations, 63; formation, 60; functions, 68, 70, 71, 86
Ministry of Foreign Trade, 22; reduction in power, 60, 61. *See also* Ministry of Foreign Economic Relations
Ministry of Tractor and Agricultural Machine Building, 61
Mitterrand, François, 47n
Monopolies, in Soviet economy, 15, 148. *See also* State monopoly of foreign trade
Montagnon, Peter, 84n
Moskoff, William, 98n
Mossberg, Walter S., 40n

National income, 99
Natural gas, exports, 11
Neo-isolationism, 29–32
Noren, James H., 96n, 101n
Norman, Peter, 46n

Obminskii, Ernst, 35n, 44
Ofer, Gur, 99n
Oil: consumption, 7; exports, 11; foreign investment in, 152; pricing system, 23; production, 6; windfall gains and losses from, 13, 24
Organization of Petroleum Exporting Countries (OPEC), 11, 58
Osnovnye polozheniia, 1987, 90, 93; budget deficit increase with, 98–99; changes in ministerial staffs, 95–96; on convertible ruble, 126; cooperatives under, 96, 98; enterprise responsibilities under, 95; implementation of comprehensive strategy for, 94; increase in republics' economic responsibilities, 108; inflationary

effects, 99, 101; price system flaws, 97–98; results, 96–97
Otsason, Rein, 112n

Patolichev, Nikolai, 58
Pavlov, Valentin, 142, 143
Peel, Quentin, 86n, 142n
Perestroika, 98, 146
Petrakov, Nikolay Ya., 27n
Pine, Art, 37n
Politburo of the Communist Party, monopoly control over economy, 20
Polozkov, Ivan, 115
Post-Soviet era: Commonwealth of Independent States, 145; economics, 150–51; foreign trade and foreign economic relations, 149–50, 151–53; market economy, 146–49; privatization, 146
Potemkin, A., 74n
Presidential Plan, Gorbachev: on confederation of republics, 139–40; draft Union treaty to increase power of republics, 139; efforts to preserve Union, 138–40; *500*-Day Plan versus, 129, 131–32; foreign economic policy, 135–38
Price system, 6; Abalkin plan for, 104; under central control, 92; CMEA, 51n; export and import, 22–23; *Osnovnye polozheniia* and, 97–98; proposed tariff system to be integrated with, 72
Privatization: *500*-Day Plan commitment to, 121; Gorbachev Presidential Plan on, 133; in post-Soviet era, 146
Productivity: capital goods, 8, 9; labor, 99, 101
Protectionism, 10; effects, 15–16; and quality of goods, 14; promotion of monopoly markets for, 14–15

Rahr, Alexander G., 31n
Rakov, Viktor, 45–46n
Reforms, Soviet: Gosplan approach to, 102–03; for integration into world economy, 2–3, 32, 33, 34–35, 130. *See also* Abalkin, Leonid, reform package; Decree on direct foreign trade rights; *500*-Day Plan; Foreign